Self-Emancipation
ON THE High Seas

Self-Emancipation
ON THE High Seas
THE *Creole* SLAVE MUTINY
OF 1841 IN LEGAL
AND DIPLOMATIC
PERSPECTIVE

William C. Gilmore

LOUISIANA STATE UNIVERSITY PRESS

BATON ROUGE

Published by Louisiana State University Press
lsupress.org

DESIGNER: Kaelin Chappell Broaddus
TYPEFACES: Bulmer MT Std, text; Etna, P22 Marcel, display

COVER ILLUSTRATION: Detail of *Night Chase of the Brigantine Slaver* Windward,
by HM Steam-Sloop Alecto (1858), by Frederick James Smyth. Reference 37945i,
Wellcome Collection.

Cataloging-in-Publication Data are available from the Library of Congress.
ISBN 978-0-8071-8486-8 (cloth) | ISBN 978-0-8071-8557-5 (epub) |
ISBN 978-0-8071-8558-2 (pdf)

To *Bob*, *Hector*, and *Sandy*,

who, in the midst of the COVID-19 pandemic,

encouraged me to undertake this project

Contents

Illustrations follow page 46.

Acknowledgments

I first became familiar with the *Creole* mutiny of November 1841 while researching the legal career of Judah P. Benjamin, the great 19th-century advocate and scholar. This resulted in a monograph, published in 2021 by Edinburgh University Press, entitled *The Confederate Jurist*. As will be seen in some detail in chapter 4 of the present study, Benjamin was a prominent figure in the Louisiana courts in the mid-1840s where the slave owners first sought compensation for the loss of their human "cargo."

Not only were the facts of this rare successful example of self-emancipation at sea compelling, but they also gave rise to a range of interesting domestic and public international law questions that had curiously attracted relatively little attention from legal scholars over the years. At a more personal level, this mutiny was centered around the then British colony of the Bahamas, the land of my birth, and placed the then uncertain norms of the international law of the sea (my first academic focus) at the heart of the resulting transatlantic dispute. The impulse to investigate the matter in detail was a strong one.

In the midst of the COVID-19 pandemic, three of my former colleagues at the Edinburgh Law School—to whom this volume is dedicated—encouraged me to prioritize this project. In undertaking the associated research, I based myself primarily at the National Library of Scotland in Edinburgh. Other library and archival collections were consulted, and visits were made to, *inter alia* (among others), the British Library and the National Archives in London and the Library of Congress in Washington, DC. In all of these institutions I was received with kindness and afforded considerable and much-appreciated assistance. I would like to take this opportunity to extend my thanks to all concerned. I also wish to acknowledge the scholars, several of whom I have never had the pleasure to meet, who when approached afforded me the assistance which I sought. Among those strangers who kindly assisted were Professor Jeffrey R. Kerr-Ritchie of Howard University and Professor Giorgio F. Colombo of Nagoya University. I am much in their debt. Others, including Emeritus Professor William C. Davis of Virginia Tech, offered welcome encouragement and support. John and Angela Ringguth were kind enough to explore the fate of the brig *Creole* while on holiday in Madeira: the *locus* of its demise in 1842.

As is my habit, the manuscript was written by hand. It was prepared for the publishers through the kindness and efficiency of my friend and former colleague Miss Lydia Lawson of Dalgety Bay, Fife. I also wish to thank the staff of Giclee UK, fine art printers of Edinburgh, for expertly enhancing the quality of the images reproduced within this volume. Finally, I wish to express my appreciation to Dr. P. R. Dotson and his colleagues at Louisiana State University Press for their assistance in bringing this project to its conclusion.

While I have derived assistance from many, the views contained in the pages which follow are mine alone. I am, of course, solely responsible for any deficiencies of style or substance which remain.

Table of Cases

Self-Emancipation
ON THE High Seas

Introduction

There is perhaps no more lamentable tale in modern Western history than the revival of the institution of slavery and its extensive utilization in the era of European colonial expansion in the New World. This barbarity formed the bedrock for, *inter alia,* plantation agriculture in the Americas from which great fortunes were made by the planters and those who serviced them and traded in their produce. The colonial powers consequently derived riches.[1] Following the American War of Independence, when cotton was king, it provided the basis for the economic well-being of much of the American South.

As Watson emphasized in his influential work *Slave Law in the Americas,* the manner in which the institution of slavery manifested itself in the law depended greatly on the underlying approach of each European colonizing power and its legal traditions.[2] In French colonial Louisiana, for example, the *Code Noir* of 1724 provided a comprehensive code of governance. The situation in the possessions of the British Crown was less uniform and more haphazard: a consequence of the devolved governance of the empire facilitated by colonial constitutional law.[3] In so-called settled colonies (a great majority), British subjects took with them both the English common law and the statute law in force at the date of settlement: "not that subsequently enacted, unless it [was] specifically extended to them."[4] As a general proposition, it can be said that from that base of reception, it was accepted that the colonizers "should, in general, be permitted to manage their own affairs and make their own laws."[5] As Watson reminds us, "[t]here was no slavery in England, hence there was no slave law in England."[6] As early as 1705, Chief Justice Holt held in *Smith* v. *Brown* that "as soon as a negro comes into England he becomes free."[7] In 1772, in the leading case of *Somerset* v. *Stewart,* Lord Mansfield opined that slavery is "so odious, that nothing can be suffered to support it, but positive law."[8] For the regulation of the institution of slavery in English colonies, therefore, statutes passed by the local legislatures were of critical relevance.

Whatever route for regulation was chosen, and irrespective of the underlying legal tradition engaged, all faced the strains and contradictions inherent in any effort to classify human beings as property. Take, for example, Louisiana—the intended destination of the enslaved central to this study. J. K. Schafer, a scholar of the jurisprudence of its Supreme Court, has remarked:

> An analysis of Louisiana Supreme Court cases about slavery provides a revealing study of bondage in the state. Slaves came before the high court for reasons as various as was the experience of slavery itself. There are cases involving slaves as criminals and as victims, as defective merchandise, as stolen goods, as self-stealers (if slaves ran away, they "stole" themselves), as concubines, as property to be seized for debts, and as objects of disputes over ownership. Slaves sued their owners for their freedom and were objects of lawsuits in which their masters or mistresses attempted to emancipate them. For a people whose very legal status was ambiguous, there was never a scarcity of slaves involved in litigation in antebellum Louisiana. Their lowly position under Louisiana law did not prevent them from occupying a significant portion of the court's time.[9]

The international trade in slaves was, as McNair reminds us, a closely related but distinct evil in the eyes of the Law of Nations;[10] one that saw countless men, women, and children abducted from Africa and subjected to the horrors of the Middle Passage. Indeed, in the painfully slow march towards abolition, this aspect of the slavery question was the first to be addressed by domestic statutes and international compacts although enforcement of the resulting prohibitions for many years remained problematic.

Given the terrible realities of slavery and the slave trade, and the vivid imagery they continue to evoke, it is understandable that there remains a keen fascination with those instances in which the enslaved rose upon their oppressors in pursuit of freedom: the Haitian Revolution of the late 18th and early 19th Centuries and Nat Turner's Rebellion in Virginia in 1831, being prominent among them. Mutinies aboard slave ships were far from uncommon. Wish noted in 1937: "The desire for liberty was manifest from the very beginning and outbreaks would occur sometimes as the ship was being loaded, or as it sailed down the Gambia River, or along the West African coast, as well as in the Middle Passage."[11] Many, as Kelley reminds us, were unsuccessful; some, as with the 1807 uprising aboard the US vessel *Independence,* resulted in extensive loss of life.[12]

Of those with a more positive outcome perhaps the best known is the case of the revolt on the Spanish schooner *La Amistad* off the coast of Cuba in the summer of 1839.[13] The enslaved rose up and gained control of the vessel and ordered that it be sailed to the coast of Africa or to an alternative destination where slavery had been abolished. By subterfuge those charged with its navigation set course for the United States, arriving off Long Island, New York, in late August. There she encountered a public vessel of the United States, the USS *Washington,* which took her to the port of New London, Connecticut, where the mutineers were detained and various legal proceedings commenced. It became something of a *cause célèbre;* one which galvanized support for the abolitionist cause in the North while engendering great disquiet in the South. It will suffice for present purposes to note that in early 1841 the matter arose for consideration by the US Supreme Court, the enslaved represented by John Quincy Adams, a former president of the United States, and Roger Sherman Baldwin, who had acted for them in earlier proceedings. The judgment of the Court, in favor of the captives, was delivered by Associate Justice Joseph Story on 9 March.[14] The same day, the British envoy in Washington wrote to the foreign secretary, then Viscount Palmerston, to inform him of the thrust of this "just and virtuous decision."[15] In his words, "By this decision the Negroes are declared to be free men, and all claim against them, whether on the part of the Spanish Minister, or of the pretended Spanish owners, is dismissed. The Negroes will be immediately set at liberty in the State of Connecticut, where they have hitherto been detained in custody waiting the event of the trial."[16]

A mere eight months later, a further successful slave mutiny took place, this time aboard the US brig *Creole.* It occurred on the high seas near the island of Abaco, part of the British colony of the Bahama Islands and proximate to the Florida coast. It forms the focus of the present study.[17] While there exist some parallels between these two examples of slave revolts at sea, there are important differences. In particular, in the case of *La Amistad,* the Supreme Court held that it was "plain beyond controversy" that the individuals concerned could not be properly classified as slaves.[18] In the words of Justice Story, "They are natives of Africa, and were kidnapped there, and were unlawfully transported to Cuba, in violation of the laws and treaties of Spain, and the most solemn edicts and declarations of that government. By those laws, and treaties, and edicts, the African slave trade is utterly abolished; the dealing in that trade is deemed a heinous crime; and the negroes thereby introduced into the dominions of Spain, are declared to be free."[19]

By way of contrast, in the case of those held in bondage on the *Creole,* it was not disputed that they were, according to the relevant laws in the United States, slaves. However, as noted in chapter 1 below, they sailed after the revolt to the British colony of the Bahamas where the institution of slavery had been abolished several years earlier. A major clash of legal cultures was the result. One American legal commentator pithily observed in 1842: "In the southern states, color is presumptive evidence of slavery; in England, humanity is conclusive evidence of freedom."[20] Similarly, in the case of the *Creole* and unlike the circumstances of *La Amistad,* the voyage did not take place in the context of, or otherwise directly relate to, the transatlantic slave trade or involve violations of the prohibitions which had come to govern it. Rather it was undertaken as part of the US coastal slave trade which remained lawful as a matter of American domestic law.[21] That said, the motivation of the enslaved to secure freedom was common to both. Judah P. Benjamin, himself a planter and slave owner, would later argue before the Supreme Court of Louisiana: "The passionate desire for liberty exists in the bosom of *every* slave—whether the recent captive, or him to whom bondage has become a habit, or was his destiny from birth."[22]

Having summarized the facts of the *Creole* revolt and the events which unfolded upon its arrival in Nassau Harbor in the Bahamas in November 1841, this study proceeds to examine the legal consequences and the diplomatic fallout which ensued. While the British colonial authorities had acknowledged the self-emancipation achieved by those who had been held in bondage on the *Creole,* the ringleaders of the revolt—some 19 in number—were detained in Nassau jail. In the uprising, there had been both injury and loss of life (though limited), and it was thought prudent to await instructions from London as to whether they should face trial in the Bahamas, be extradited to the United States, or have their liberty confirmed. The great majority walked free, many leaving shortly thereafter for Jamaica. Chapter 2 examines the detailed consideration of these matters by the imperial law officers, by British ministers, by senior officials, and within the Westminster Parliament. This, in turn, set the stage for the eventual liberation of the 17 surviving ringleaders (two having died in prison) by order of the Vice-Admiralty Court of the Bahamas in the spring of 1842. This crystalized the nature and scope of the resulting bilateral dispute between the United Kingdom and the United States.

Anglo-American relations were under considerable strain throughout the 1830s, and the *Creole* affair added a further and unwelcome element of complexity to that important diplomatic relationship. Chapter 3 examines the initial efforts to address the range of irritants that had arisen between the two countries, including those flowing from the *Creole* incident. That task fell to US Secretary of State Daniel Webster and Lord Ashburton, a special emissary appointed by the British government.

They engaged in intensive negotiations in Washington, DC, between April and August of 1842. The focus of the analysis is on those aspects of the discussions most relevant to the *Creole* affair, namely extradition and the affording of greater security to American vessels navigating the hazardous waters of the Bahamas. The outcome, as will be seen, was more favorable to the position of the United Kingdom than that of the United States.

The Webster–Ashburton negotiations had left to one side the contentious issue of the payment of compensation to the slave owners of those aboard the *Creole* for the loss of their human "property." That is the focus of chapter 4 of this work. It commences with the efforts of the slavers to secure recompense from their respective insurers which had denied liability. Extensive litigation in Louisiana was the consequence. In most cases, the supreme court of that state would find in favor of the insurance companies whereupon those out-of-pocket looked to the US Federal authorities for assistance. After a gap of several years, Britain and America agreed to a form of international arbitration. The interstate dispute concerning the *Creole,* one of many to be submitted to this *ad hoc* arbitral commission, was framed in terms of the international law of the sea. In early January 1855, its umpire, Joshua Bates, held in favor of the United States. Compensation to the slavers and others with a property interest in the lost "cargo" was awarded and promptly paid. The chapter subjects this judicial ruling to critical scrutiny and raises doubts as to its legal merits and precedential value.

The study concludes, in chapter 5, with a series of reflections on the most successful mutiny in the history of the American coastal slave trade and its significance legally, diplomatically, and (to the extent known) for its principal actors. This is an intriguing and complex example of the quest for freedom and its aftermath. It deserves serious consideration in the continuing efforts to address and understand the abolition of slavery in the Americas.

Chapter 1

Flight to Freedom

IT'S BETTER IN
THE BAHAMAS

On Monday, October 25, 1841, the American-owned and registered merchantman, the brig[1] *Creole,* departed Richmond, Virginia, *en route* to New Orleans, Louisiana, under the command of Captain Robert Ensor. This was a long-established trading route and one which the *Creole* had undertaken on several previous occasions.[2] The Captain was assisted by a first and second mate (Zephaniah Gifford and Lucius Stevens respectively) and a crew of six.[3] The vessel itself was relatively new and of common design. Kerr-Ritchie remarked, "It was constructed in the shipyards of Richmond in 1840. With a burden of 187 and 25/95 tons, the brig was ninety-five feet long, twenty-five feet and six inches wide with a depth of eight feet and nine inches. The vessel had one deck and two masts. The stern was square. A lady's figure adorned the head of the ship."[4] In the days which followed, the *Creole* made a number of stops to take on additional cargo.[5] By the time it proceeded to the open seas on Sunday, October 31, it had on board a quantity of tobacco in boxes, in excess of 130 enslaved persons,[6] and several passengers. Of the human cargo, slightly less than half were female.

It is important to recall that while the United States had taken steps
years earlier to abolish the transatlantic slave trade, the internal trade in
slaves, by land or sea, had not been similarly treated.[7] Aaron Vail, the
American Chargé d'Affaires in London[8] explained the resulting situation
to the British foreign secretary[9] on 20 September 1834:

> Although the United States, with a view to the prevention of the African
> slave trade, prohibit[s] under the severest penalties, the introduction of
> slaves from foreign parts into the territories of the Union, they yet permit
> the free transfer of colored persons born and held in servitude in the
> country, from one section of it to another; and that, in consequence of
> this, the case daily occurs of owners of that species of property travelling
> with their servants through the different States, or, with a view to the
> formation of agricultural establishments, removing their slaves, by land
> or sea, from one State to the other where slavery continues to exist under
> their respective laws.[10]

In the case at hand, both the ports of origin and of destination were
located in so-called slave states. Indeed, at that time New Orleans had a
thriving market for the "sale" of the enslaved, which catered to the demand in Louisiana and elsewhere in the Deep South (see fig. 1).

As the *Creole* wound its way south along the US Atlantic coast, its
human "cargo" was not subject to a particularly rigorous security regime.
Eight members of the ship's company were later to attest that:

> the male and female slaves were divided—the men were placed in the
> forward hold of said vessel, excepting Lewis, an old servant of Thomas
> McCargo, who was permitted to remain in the cabin, and the women in
> the hold aft, excepting six female house servants taken into the cabin—
> and between the aforesaid slaves was the cargo of said vessel, consisting
> of boxes of tobacco; that the aforesaid slaves were permitted to go on
> deck, but the men were not allowed at night to go into the hold aft where
> the women were.[11]

Responsibility for the supervision of the enslaved persons was a shared one and primarily involved William Henry Merritt (a passenger), John R. Hewell (a passenger and slave owner), and Captain Ensor.[12]

The voyage was uneventful until Sunday, November 7. That evening, "when about one hundred and thirty miles to the north-north east of the Hole in the Wall"[13]—a then curious coastal geological feature well known to mariners and the site of a lighthouse[14]—"the captain, supposing the vessel was nearer Abaco than she really was, ordered the brig laid to, which was accordingly done, there being a fresh breeze, and the sky a little hazy, with trade-clouds flying."[15] More precisely the location was put at latitude 27°46' north, and 75°20' west. This is to be found in the upper right-hand quadrant of the map reproduced in figure 2. Shortly thereafter, a group of male slaves (at least 19 in number) rose in revolt in an effort to secure their freedom from bondage.[16] As Edward Everett,[17] the American envoy to London, was later to remark, in the ensuing melee the rebels "wounded the captain dangerously, and the chief mate and two of the crew severely, and killed a passenger named John Hewell, the owner of part of the slaves, who was employed with the officers in resisting the mutiny. The slaves, soon obtaining the entire possession of the vessel, compelled the officers to steer her to the port of Nassau, in the British Island of New Providence, and remained undisputed masters of her till her arrival at that place on the morning of the 9th."[18]

The choice of Nassau was both convenient and inspired. It was the chief settlement and seat of government of the British colony of the Bahamas—an archipelago of hundreds of islands, rocks, and cays stretching southeastward in an arc from Grand Bahama, proximate to the coast of Florida, to the near of the Windward Passage, a gateway to the Caribbean Sea.[19] Fortuitously, at the time of the uprising, the *Creole*, as noted above, was relatively close to the island of Abaco, itself one of the Bahama islands.

The choice of the Bahamas was inspired because of the very different stance adopted by the British Empire at that time to the institution of slavery. The British connection with the territory dates back to the earliest times of European transatlantic exploration and expansion, but it was only in 1729 that the Crown "assumed direct control."[20] As a matter of colonial constitutional law, the Bahamas was considered a settled colony[21] by virtue of which the underlying basic law was the common law of England "and the statute law in force at the time of settlement—not that subsequently enacted, unless specifically extended to them."[22] In the case of the Bahamas, further clarification of the extent of the reception of English law was provided in the Declaratory Act of 1799.[23]

In the Bahamas, as in the other British West Indian colonies, the institution of slavery was initially an acknowledged part of the legal framework. For many years, however, the numbers held in bondage were relatively small in comparison with the larger plantation-based economies of, for instance, Jamaica or Barbados. A significant expansion of slave ownership took place due to the arrival of a substantial number of loyalists in the wake of the American War of Independence. Consequently, in a total population of 11,300 by 1789, people of color greatly outnumbered the white population. Of these, 7,500 were enslaved and 500 free.[24] The non-white population was to be further enhanced as a consequence of initiatives taken to suppress the African slave trade. As Lord McNair reminds us, this "was made criminal throughout the British Empire . . . as from January 1807 by a statute of 1806, strengthened by later statutes."[25] Such prohibitions were, in turn, policed by the Royal Navy. Those freed were taken to convenient ports in the Empire; the Bahamas, due to its geographic location, was a frequent beneficiary.

Within the United Kingdom, as is well known, pressure gradually mounted for the abolition of the institution of slavery itself. This culminated with the enactment by the Imperial Parliament at Westminster of the Slavery Abolition Act 1833,[26] which entered into force on 1 August 1834. By virtue of this enactment, slaves in the Bahamas became formally free as of that date. They were, however, subject to a controversial four-year apprenticeship system which expired in 1838, upon which there came a more concrete realization of emancipation. This radical initiative was underpinned by a system of compensation. Perversely, as it now seems, this provided recompense to the slave owner for loss of property and not to the enslaved for loss of liberty. The compensation commission charged with oversight of this task kept meticulous records which have been digitized in a unique database created by University College London.[27] This source has been interrogated by Saunders with respect to the Bahamas. It reveals: "The total number of pay-outs to former slave-owners was 1,057 in the amount of £126,848.70 in compensation for 10,087 slaves."[28]

This was the broad context and clash of legal cultures which greeted the approach of the *Creole* to Nassau harbor on the morning of 9 November 1841. As was common practice, it was met by a pilot boat, to ensure its safe entry. It came to anchor "at the west end of the harbor, just within the bar, and but a short distance from the northern shore of the harbor, and about one mile from the public buildings of the town of Nassau."[29] The quarantine boat also came alongside. Gifford, the (former) first mate was permitted by those in control of the *Creole* to accompany the quarantine officer to the shore where he was taken directly to the office of the American consul (see fig. 3).[30]

That diplomatic post was occupied by John F. Bacon, who had assumed office in March of the previous year. Having been briefed by Gifford on what had transpired on the voyage from Richmond, Bacon determined that the two of them should immediately take the short journey to Government House and seek a meeting with the governor.[31] The post of governor, the local representative of the Crown, which stood at the apex of political and military power within the territory, had been held since 1837 by Sir Francis Cockburn. A former army officer, who had served for many years in various British possessions in Canada, he was also a seasoned colonial administrator.[32]

The governor quickly made himself available and was briefed by them on the circumstances surrounding the unexpected arrival of this US-flagged vessel. Bacon also made a verbal request for intervention which, at Cockburn's request, was formally submitted in written form. It was short and direct but limited in scope. It read, in its substantive part: "Having had detailed to your excellency the particulars of the mutiny and murder on board the American brig Creole by slaves on board said brig, I have now to request that your excellency will be pleased not to suffer any of the slaves on board to land until further investigations can be made."[33] Shortly thereafter, the local colonial secretary, C. R. Nesbitt, informed the consul that, in fulfillment of the object of that request, "his excellency has ordered a military party on board of said brig."[34] To that end, a detachment from the Second West India Regiment from the nearby barracks boarded the *Creole*.[35] In the meantime, Bacon busied himself with various tasks, including securing medical treatment for Captain Ensor and others who had suffered injury.[36]

Given the then primitive state of communications, reliant on written dispatches carried by sea, the governor was not able to seek timely instructions from London. Rather, he had to draw on his own experience and best judgment and the advice of other locally based officials. Perhaps fortunately, there had been several previous occasions in which US merchant vessels with slaves aboard had been driven by force of weather or navigational misfortune into the Bahamas and other British colonies such as Bermuda.[37] The most recent instance had taken place only one year earlier and involved the American schooner *Hermosa* with 38 slaves on board. It, too, was on a voyage from Richmond to New Orleans when shipwrecked on the island of Abaco. The ship's company and the enslaved were rescued and taken to Nassau where the latter were set free despite the protest of the American consul.[38] The other leading postemancipation act incident, involving the vessel *Enterprize* and the treatment of the slaves aboard it by the authorities of Bermuda[39] (discussed in greater detail at a later stage of this study),[40] also pointed in the direction of freedom. By way of illustration, on 25 May 1839, the Colonial Office in Downing Street sent a circular dispatch to relevant territories, including the Bahamas, on the outcome of the government's consideration of US demands for compensation following the freeing of slaves aboard the *Comet,* the *Encomium,* and the *Enterprize*—all US flagged merchantmen. The first two had been shipwrecked in the Bahamas in the years prior to the abolition of slavery. The *Enterprize,* in contrast, was driven by adverse weather, and related issues, into Hamilton Harbor in Bermuda in 1835.[41] The dispatch attached two treasury minutes setting out in detail the grounds upon which it had been agreed to pay compensation with respect to the first two instances but to reject similar demands in relation to the *Enterprize*.[42] In so doing, the Colonial Office felt that the respective territorial governments "should be in possession of the reasons which have guided" these decisions lest similar events transpire in the future.[43] For present purposes, it is sufficient to note that a central guiding principle was that no claim for indemnification of loss would be entertained in respect of "other Slaves thrown within the British Jurisdiction in the Colonial Possessions or otherwise subsequently to the Abolition of Slavery throughout the British Dominions, and availing themselves of the protection of the British Laws."[44]

While these incidents provided Cockburn with some guidance, none were exact precedents. The *Creole* was unique in the sense that it was the first case to arise in a British territory out of a successful revolt by enslaved persons who, on the high seas, had committed acts of violence in seeking to secure their freedom. The governor decided to consult with his executive council, established pursuant to the Letters Patent of 12 January 1841, and convened an emergency session on the same morning. Bacon was thereafter requested to attend the meeting which was still in progress to learn of the decisions which had been reached.[45] He was then read a prepared statement in the following terms:

> We wish to state to you, as the representative of the American Government, that the circumstances detailed to the Governor this morning in your presence, respecting the events which took place on board of the American brig Creole on the night and subsequently to the 7th of November, have been given all possible consideration to by the Governor and Council, by whom the following decisions have been come to:
>
> 1st That the courts of law here have no jurisdiction over the alleged offences.
>
> 2d But that as an information had been lodged before his excellency the Governor, charging the crime of murder to have been committed on board of the said vessel while on the high seas, it was expedient that the parties implicated in so grave a charge should not

be allowed to go at large, and that an investigation ought therefore to be made into the charges, and examinations taken on oath, when if it should appear that the original information was correct, and that a murder had actually been committed, that all the parties implicated in such crime, or in any other acts of violence, should be detained here until reference could be made to the Secretary of State to ascertain whether the parties detained should be delivered over to the American Government or not, and if not, how otherwise to be disposed of.

3d   That so soon as such examinations should be taken, all the persons on board of the Creole, not implicated in any of the offences alleged to have been committed on board of that vessel, must be released from further restraint.

4th   That a detailed account of what has taken place should be transmitted to the British minister at Washington.[46]

As Bacon was later to inform US Secretary of State Daniel Webster, the governor then asked if he was satisfied. Bacon replied that "so far as to sending on board troops and directing an examination, I was, but declined a further answer at that time."[47] As will be seen below, this somewhat delphic and abbreviated response was, days later, to prove to be a source of both difficulty and misunderstanding.

In furtherance of the decisions of the governor in council, the police magistrate (Robert Duncombe) and a justice of the peace (J. J. Burnside) boarded the Creole later on Tuesday, November 9, and commenced a process of securing sworn affidavits from select members of the ship's company and its passengers. As has been noted elsewhere, "these official inquiries were aimed at finding out exactly who was responsible for the death of John Hewell, who caused the injuries to the officers and crew, and what had occurred during the uprising."[48] These interviews continued until the following Friday[49] but did not extend to any of the enslaved.[50] The outcome was a list of 19 slaves identified as leaders of the mutiny and thus suspects in the "murder" and associated acts of violence. These individuals were, on the same day, removed to the nearby Nassau jail to await the decision of the relevant authorities in London as to their longer-term fate (see fig. 4). At that time, the attorney general of the Bahamas, G. C. Anderson, informed those who had been so detained, that "if they wished copies of the informations, they should be furnished with them, and they should also be at liberty, if they thought proper, to have witnesses examined in refutation of the charges made against them, with all of which they expressed themselves to be satisfied."[51] A full accounting of the identities of those in question was provided to the US consul by the colonial secretary on November 26. By that time, one (George Grandy) had perished from the wounds he had sustained in the course of the uprising, and another (Adam Carney) had died in custody, seemingly from natural causes.[52] The full listing was as follows:

Madison Washington
Ben Johnstone or Blacksmith
Elijah Morris
Doctor Ruffin
George Grandy, dead, by a wound in the head
Richard Butler
Phil Jones
Robert Lumpkins or Lumpley
Peter Smallwood
Warner Smith
Walter Brown
Adam Carney, dead
Horace Beverley
America
Addison Tyler
William Jenkins
Pompey Garrison
George Basden
George Portlock—Total 19[53]

The issue of the future of the remaining slaves aboard the *Creole* was also to be determined on Friday the 12th though in circumstances which were to be much contested.[54] What is clear is that in a note handed that day at 12 noon by the consul to the office of the governor, the former expressed significant security concerns. In his words: "On proceeding to go on board the brig Creole, with the magistrates this morning, I saw a large collection of persons on the shore nearest the vessel, and many in boats; and was, at the same time, informed that the moment the troops should be withdrawn from the brig, an attempt would be made to board her by force. I was further informed an attempt had already been made. I have, therefore, to request your excellency will take such measures as you may deem proper for the protection of the said vessel and cargo."[55] The governor immediately replied. Having first expressed his incredulity that any locals would act in such an improper manner, he assured the US consul that "should such an unauthorized attempt be made, I shall be quite ready to use every authorized means for preventing it."[56]

As it happened, the governor was in formal session with his executive council, and Mr. Bacon was verbally invited to attend. Upon doing so, he was informed that, in the light of his communication, it had been decided "to direct the attorney general with the provost marshal, and as many police-men as he might deem necessary to proceed to the brig, first have the troops and prisoners removed on shore, see that no violence was committed by the people collected, and also that no impediment be given on board the vessel to the slaves landing, if they should desire to do so (he calling them passengers)."[57] These instructions were carried out that afternoon. The great majority of those who had previously been held captive came ashore, a small number electing to remain on board with a view to continuing their journey to New Orleans notwithstanding the life of servitude which would result.[58] As the consul subsequently informed Secretary of State Webster, they "came on shore in a body, and proceeded to the office of the superintendent of the police, accompanied by between one and two thousand people. I understand . . . that the superintendent registered all their names, and informed them they were all free to go where they pleased."[59] In this manner, their self-emancipation was acknowledged. Many left for the British West Indian colony of Jamaica in the following days, the remainder blending into the local population as they commenced the rebuilding of their lives in freedom.[60]

It is of importance to note one particular curiosity at this stage. It will be recalled that in his communication of November 12 to the governor, in which he had raised his concerns, Bacon mentioned that an attempt to board the *Creole* by force "had already been made."[61] It is, however, by no means clear from the extensive documentary record generated in Nassau in November of 1841 what facts this allegation seeks to engage. Some commentators, including Jervey and Huber, have concluded that it is in fact a reference to a plan, to which Bacon was a party and to which the colonial authorities were not alerted in advance, to utilize members of the crew of two American flag merchant vessels then in Nassau Harbor to liberate the *Creole* from the British "and conduct her to Indian Key, where there was a United States vessel of war."[62] While, at first sight, this might seem far-fetched, it gained traction from the fact that it was set out in some detail in the joint formal sworn protest lodged by various members of the crew and passengers upon the arrival of the *Creole* in New Orleans in December of 1841.[63] This attempt was, they claimed, thwarted by the West India Regiment troops on board by a threat to use force: "It was that interference which prevented aid from being rendered by the American sailors in Nassau, and caused the loss of slaves to their owners."[64] This narrative, largely absent from the formal diplomatic record surrounding the *Creole* incident,[65] was accepted by the umpire, Joshua Bates, in his January 1855 arbitral award intended to afford a final settlement to the dispute between the USA and Great Britain over this matter.[66] This decision is afforded detailed treatment at a later stage of this study.[67]

In the period after the disembarkation of the former slaves, it became clear that the British and American authorities had very different views as to the factual circumstances which had given rise to the events of that Friday and as to the appropriate course of action which should now be taken. The American position crystalized over the course of the weekend. That Saturday, the US consul took several sworn depositions from selected members of the crew, a passenger, and William Woodside, master of the American bark *Louisa,* then in Nassau Harbor, who had been intimately involved in discussions with Bacon since the arrival of the *Creole.*[68]

He then set about the task of formulating a further note to Sir Francis Cockburn dated "Monday morning, November 14, 1841."[69] It was, in the main, a formal diplomatic protest at the freeing of the former slaves the previous Friday. It reads in relevant part:

> Against the manner of their liberation, and all the proceedings which ultimately effected it, on the part of her Majesty's officers and subjects, I deem it my duty to enter my solemn protest; and, also, on behalf of the chief mate, now, and then, in command of the said vessel, also to protest.
>
> These slaves, as I view the case, while they were under the American flag, and regularly cleared from one slaveholding State to another, within the United States, were as much a portion of the cargo of the said brig, as the tobacco and other articles on board; and whether on the high seas, or in an English port, does not change their character; and, that her Majesty's Government had not the right to interfere with, or control, the officers of an American vessel, thus circumstanced, in such a course as might be necessary and proper to secure such property from being lost to the owners.[70]

The consul further requested that the previous decision to retain the ringleaders in custody pending receipt of further instructions from the British government be reconsidered. In particular, he requested that the prisoners be placed aboard the *Creole* upon its departure to New Orleans so they might be tried under American law.[71] The ready availability of witnesses at such US-based judicial proceedings was much emphasized.[72]

In his reply of the following day, the governor expressed his disappointment at the position which Bacon had adopted. He also stressed that "as our intentions were throughout made known to you previously to being acted upon, without calling forth any objections on your part, we could not but consider that you acquiesced in them."[73] The governor also noted that the American characterization of the role of the attorney general while aboard the vessel did "not accord with the official report thereof, made to me by that officer."[74] He enclosed that report, dated November 13, for Bacon's information. In it, the attorney general confirmed that he had informed the slaves not identified as having been implicated in the revolt that "as far as the authorities of the island were concerned, all restrictions on their movements were removed."[75] He also noted that the decision taken by the great majority to go ashore "was their own free and voluntary act" and that "neither myself nor any of the authorities of the colony then on board interfered in the slightest manner to induce them to take that step."[76] Finally, the governor declined to deliver over to the US consul those then in prison "for the purpose of being secured and sent to America for trial."[77]

The contours of an interstate dispute between Great Britain and the United States were thus set and nothing further of consequence transpired prior to the departure of the *Creole en route* to New Orleans on November 19. Cockburn would have been justified in reflecting at that stage that he had played at least some part—albeit a controversial one—in the long history of efforts to secure an end to the maritime trade in human beings. In that sense, he added to something of a family tradition initiated by one of his older and more distinguished siblings. Admiral Sir George Cockburn—best known in the Americas for his role in the sacking of Washington and the burning of the White House in 1814—was a central figure in the events giving rise to the leading English case of *Forbes v. Cochrane and Cockburn* [78] It will be recalled that in 1824, the Court of Kings Bench held that the moment a slave boards a British ship of war outside of the territorial waters of the territory from which he or she has escaped that person becomes subject exclusively to the law of England and is thus free.[79]

Chapter 2

The Mutineers in Nassau Jail

TRIAL, EXTRADITION, OR LIBERTY?

Even prior to the departure of the *Creole* from Nassau, Sir Francis Cockburn had written both to the British minister to the United States in Washington[1]—as envisaged by the 9 November decision of the Governor in Council treated in the previous chapter—and to Lord Stanley, the Secretary of State for the Colonies in London.[2] The latter dispatch, dated November 17, 1841—though delivered only on December 27—and containing extensive enclosures set out the "situation of some difficulty and delicacy" with which he had been confronted and sought further instructions on a range of related matters.[3]

Of particular concern to the governor was the need for the timely receipt of "positive instructions as to the disposal of those whom . . . I have taken upon me to detain in custody until Her Majesty's pleasure concerning their disposal should be made known."[4] More generally he was anxious to receive assurances that the measures he had taken "are approved and confirmed by Her Majesty's Government" and to underline that there had been no timely protest of his actions by the American authorities. He wrote, "Your Lordship will observe that no remonstrance or protest of any kind was made by the American Consul here or those belonging to the Ship, until long after the Negroes had gone on shore but on the contrary I had reason to consider that he and they fully acquiesced in everything that took place."[5] Given the grave nature of the incident it was not long before the colonial secretary brought the matter to the attention of the Earl of Aberdeen, the then foreign secretary.[6] In so doing the Colonial Office remarked "that in a question of so much inter-national importance he [Lord Stanley] has thought it right to call upon the Law Officers of the Crown for their opinion."[7]

In parallel, as noted in the previous chapter, Mr. Bacon had taken steps to provide Secretary of State Webster with detailed information of his view as to what had transpired in Nassau, the fundamental thrust of which was that the slaves had been liberated "through the interference of the authorities of the colony."[8] In addition, upon arrival in New Orleans, members of the ship's company had formulated a lengthy sworn protest,[9] the text of which soon became public. Something of a political storm "erupted,"[10] causing much-animated discussion in the press and in American political circles.[11] As Vega has remarked: "Britain's actions were not well received in the United States. Southerners, in particular, resented the British for intervening in a situation that they believed to be an American issue."[12] As early as 28 December 1841, the British minister in Washington, Henry S. Fox, wrote to warn the foreign secretary that "an impression prevails here that the 19 negroes detained at Nassau, charged with the murder on board the *Creole* of one of the American slave-owners, will be delivered up for trial in the United States."[13]

It was thus within a swiftly evolving and increasingly heated political context that the Law Officers of the Crown set about their work. This development has on occasion been a source of some confusion for commentators.[14] Put simply, a referral to the law officers was then—and remains—a standard procedure by which British governments can obtain formal written legal advice on issues of difficulty. Though the resulting opinions have often been highly influential,[15] they are not legally binding. Such opinions are treated as confidential and, by convention, are rarely, if ever, published at the time.

It was the then standard practice to seek the collective advice of three such law officers on matters of a complex international nature:[16] namely, the Attorney General of England and Wales, the Solicitor General of England and Wales, and the Queen's Advocate. The latter office was last held by Sir Travers Twiss, who resigned in 1872 following a matrimonial scandal.[17] It has since fallen into desuetude.

In January of 1842, the attorney general was Sir Frederick Pollock,[18] and the solicitor general was Sir William Follett.[19] They had much in common. Both had attended Trinity College in Cambridge and thereafter qualified as English barristers. Both held the rank of Queen's Counsel (QC) and were members of parliament. Neither had an extensive background in legal matters of an international character. Sir John Dodson was the Queen's Advocate, a position he had held since 1834.[20] An Oxford graduate, he was both an advocate in Doctors' Commons and a barrister.[21] He also had extensive experience in admiralty law, which was highly relevant to the facts of the *Creole* incident.

While the law officers had, in the years prior to 1842, been called upon to opine with some frequency on matters connected with slavery and the consequences of its abolition within the Empire,[22] the *Creole* incident raised some highly unusual questions. In particular, this had been a rare and successful uprising on board a foreign vessel on the high seas which had been accomplished through the use of force, resulting in both injury and death. Those involved had voluntarily entered a British territory and then languished in Nassau jail awaiting a determination of their fate. Unsurprisingly, three of the six questions posed to the law officers by the secretary of state for the colonies directly engaged with this central concern.

As seen in the previous chapter, the crime of murder had been alleged. Was such a charge, in the circumstances of this case, one which could properly be brought before a court in the Bahamas or elsewhere within the Queen's dominions? In short, did the courts have jurisdiction? As we have seen, on 9 November 1841, the governor in council had answered in the negative.[23] This was the first question posed to the law officers and properly so. *The Spectator* commented on 22 January 1842, "With regard to the alleged crime, there arose two questions—first, the question of jurisdiction: second, the question whether the crime has been committed? The first question must be first decided."[24]

All countries assert prescriptive or legislative jurisdiction regarding crime on the basis of territoriality—that is, where the acts complained of took place within its territory or, in some instances, where those acts produced effects within that territory.[25] In the 19th century, common law countries were particularly closely wedded to this principle, and reliance on other grounds permitted by customary international law, such as the nationality of the perpetrator, was rarely invoked.[26] It is of relevance to note for present purposes that then, as now, the obligations of a national criminal justice system extended to encompass acts committed on one of its vessels in a maritime context. As a matter of customary international law such flag state jurisdiction on the high seas was considered to be exclusive in nature.[27] Viewed in this context, it was no surprise that, in their opinion of 29 January 1842—reproduced in full in appendix 1—the view as to jurisdiction articulated by the governor in council the previous November was, in effect, upheld. The law officers concluded: "They may be chargeable with the Crime of Murder, but as they are not British Subjects and the Crime was not committed on board a British Vessel, they cannot be tried by a British Tribunal for the Offence."[28]

They next turned their attention to a recognized exception to the principles of both territoriality and exclusive flag state jurisdiction, namely piracy. As Bantekas reminds us, piracy *jure gentium* "is subject to universal jurisdiction under both customary international law and Art.105 UN Convention on the Law of the Sea."[29] Indeed, at the relevant time, piracy alone was recognized in customary law as falling within the ambit of this principle.[30]

While the exact definition of piracy in international law remained open to some debate throughout the 19th century—and beyond—there was some measure of consensus as to its various core features.[31] If considered to constitute a piratical act, associated jurisdictional issues are reduced to near nothingness. Lord McNair has remarked, "The main consequence of this unique character is that nearly all the problems of jurisdiction which hamper the proper prosecution and punishment of other crimes of an international character disappear, and piracy is justiciable in the courts of any State, whether or not the particular State is affected by the allegedly piratical acts and whether connected by ties of nationality with the accused or not."[32]

Could the *Creole* incident be so characterized? In his dispatch to the colonial secretary dated 17 November 1841, Sir Francis Cockburn noted that he had been unable "fully to satisfy [himself] on this point, though the Law Officers here think it was not."[33] He thus requested clarification. The imperial law officers agreed with their counterparts in the Bahamas: "It appears to us that the Act of the Negroes in compelling by violence the Crew of the *Creole* to alter her course and take her into a British Port does not either by the General Law of Nations or by the Municipal Law of this Country amount to the Crime of Piracy, and therefore that it is not cognizable by any English Tribunal."

Having reached the above conclusions it was a straightforward matter to dispose of the second question with which they had been presented— that is, whether the Bahamas and the United States enjoyed concurrent jurisdiction with respect to the alleged offense. In their view, "having been committed by Persons subject to the American Law on board an American Ship, against the Persons of American Citizens it is exclusively cognizable by the Criminal Tribunals of the United States."

In the light of these determinations, the next issue of practical and legal significance was whether or not the British authorities were bound as a matter of international law, and able as a matter of domestic law, to deliver those in Nassau jail, upon demand from the American government, to the US for trial in that country. If so, did the British authorities possess any discretion in relation to such surrender? These were the central features embodied in the third question presented to the law officers.

In international law and practice, the standard procedure is for the state where the alleged criminal offense took place to seek the extradition of the accused person from the foreign jurisdiction in which that individual was physically located.[34] In the 1840s, the law relating to extradition was still relatively embryonic. It was, however, clear that if a bilateral treaty providing for surrender was in place between the requesting and requested states, and the offense in question fell within the ambit of that international agreement, extradition would be mandatory. There was at the relevant time no such treaty relationship subsisting between the United States and Great Britain. In the view of the law officers, it followed that the government was thus not legally obligated to honor any request for surrender by the American authorities.

This, however, did not fully dispose of the issue at hand. As a matter of customary international law, while a state is obligated to extradite only by virtue of the operation of a relevant treaty provision, it also permits surrender in the absence of the same. This process is commonly known as *ad hoc* extradition.[35] It was to this that Dodson, Pollock, and Follett turned their attention. To them, the crux of the matter was whether the law of England imposed any obstacle in the way of satisfying any such request. It was, in turn, "a question on which we have felt very considerable difficulty." In their examination of the law and practice on this point (in both countries), they found contradictory precedents and approaches. On balance, "and after a most minute investigation of the various conflicting authorities and an anxious consideration of this important subject," they concluded that the government "cannot legally direct the delivery up of the persons now in custody in the Bahamas to the Authorities of the United States." They did, however, leave open the possibility that there might exist a local law in the colony of the Bahamas with a bearing on this matter.

In contrast to matters relating to the fate of the 17 still in custody, the law officers dealt with the circumstances through which the remainder of the enslaved persons on the *Creole* secured their liberty only obliquely and in brief. This arose for consideration in two overlapping ways. First, they had been requested to address whether Sir Francis Cockburn and the colonial authorities in the Bahamas had acted in accordance with both international and domestic law in dealing with the *Creole* incident. They concluded, on the basis of the information provided, that they had. While in some respects the failure to address this matter in detail might seem surprising, the position of the law officers on the arrival of enslaved

persons on the territory of the empire post-emancipation had been clarified in previous opinions.[36] As the secretary of state for the colonies was
to subsequently state to the governor, British officials had no hesitation
in concluding that the enslaved "being within the limits of British territory within which limits the condition of Slavery is not recognised by
law, and being charged with no crime they voluntarily quitted the vessel
on board of which there was no legal power to detain them."[37] Second,
they were directed to consider the legal merits of the protest lodged by
the American consul in Nassau in his letter to Governor Cockburn on
14 November 1841.[38] As was seen in the previous chapter, the essence of
the position adopted by Bacon was that the liberation of those on board
had been secured through the interference of the colonial authorities to
which they had no right. The law officers disagreed: "The Slaves were
not liberated by the British Authorities, nor does it appear that any Control was exercised by them, in this respect over the Crew of the Ship." In
short, the position taken by the consul was regarded as being based on
"a misapprehension of the facts."

As was noted earlier in this study, a small number of the enslaved persons elected to remain on the *Creole* and return with it to New Orleans.
Was it lawful for the colonial authorities to permit a vessel with such
persons on board to depart Nassau Harbor and, if so, was it incumbent
upon them to ascertain whether such persons did so "of their own free
and unbiased will." In a brief response, the law officers adopted the view
that the authorities acted lawfully in granting the vessel clearance to return to the United States and that they were not obligated to ensure that
the remaining enslaved persons were returning "of their own free will
or otherwise."

On January 31, but two days after the finalization of the opinion of
the law officers, Lord Stanley wrote to Sir Francis Cockburn enclosing
a copy. He concluded the dispatch as follows: "It affords me much pleasure to be enabled to convey to you the assurance that HMs Govt entirely
approve of the course which you have taken in the difficult circumstances
in which you were called upon to act upon your own responsibility."[39]

By this stage, the events surrounding the *Creole* incident had started to attract media attention in the United Kingdom and generate public and political debate.[40] Illustrating its growing significance, on January 21, *The Times,* the then principal newspaper of record in the UK, had seen fit to reproduce the lengthy New Orleans protest, made upon the arrival of the vessel in New Orleans, in full.[41] Of special interest for present purposes is the debate which took place in the House of Lords, the upper chamber of the British Parliament, on Monday 14 February 1842.[42] There, the foreign secretary, Lord Aberdeen, clarified the decision which had been taken, in the wake of the law officers' opinion, on the fate of those still held in the jail at Nassau. He clarified that "they had satisfied themselves that by the laws of this country there is no machinery or authority for bringing those persons to trial for mutiny and murder, still less for detaining them in custody." Instructions had accordingly been issued to the governor that, unless there was a local law in force within the colony relevant to this matter, and justifying a different approach, the prisoners should be released from custody forthwith. Unusually, the ensuing contributions to the debate came exclusively from the leading lawyers, then members of the House.[43] They were at one in focusing on the issue of extradition. All were of the view that, in the absence of a treaty obligation requiring surrender and relevant domestic implementing legislation, there was no basis in law for surrendering Madison Washington and his comrades for trial in the United States. Indeed, Lord Denman, a former lord chief justice, had come prepared to warn ministers of the consequences of any such prisoner transfer. In his words, "they could not seize or detain aliens seeking refuge here without subjecting themselves to actions for damages for false imprisonment, and without further incurring the risk of a still heavier and more awful responsibility; for if a man attempted to seize an alien under such authority he might resist, and if death ensued, he would be justified in inflicting it, while those who ordered his arrest and detention would be liable to be tried for murder." As the foreign secretary was later to stress to the American minister in London, these views, "though not delivered from the judgment-seat, was invested with judicial solemnity, and it was perfectly unanimous, embracing every description of political party and opinion."[44]

As of early February, no American diplomatic *démarche* had been received in London giving the impression that the administration of President Tyler was making haste slowly. On the 9th of that month, Lord Aberdeen wrote to Lord Ashburton—who was preparing for an important and complex set of negotiations with the United States.[45] Aberdeen stated, "It is extraordinary that we still hear nothing of the *Creole,* but we shall be prepared."[46]

In truth, the government in Washington, DC, had been far from inactive. Its initial focus, however, had been to address a domestic audience in advance of engaging directly with London. In that context, the president had, in mid-January, presented the Senate with extensive documentation concerning this then high-profile incident.[47] Exactly one month later,[48] the same body was presented with the text of the formal instructions which had been sent by Secretary of State Webster to the American Minister in Great Britain. Upon seeing the text reproduced in the press Henry Fox, the British envoy in Washington, forwarded its contents to London and informed Lord Aberdeen that it had been received in the Senate "as might be expected, with great applause by the southern and slave-holding members."[49]

Dated 29 January 1841, it set out at considerable length the facts surrounding this "very serious occurrence."[50] The American position is considered in greater detail in the following chapter. It will suffice for present purposes to note that it takes grave exception to the acts of the colonial authorities concerning both the general liberation of the enslaved persons on board and their approach to the imprisoned suspected ringleaders of the revolt. As to the latter, Webster surmised that the British were unlikely "to undertake their trial and punishment" and questioned the utility, in practice, of returning them to the United States for trial. Consequently "[o]ne of the highest offences known to human law is thus likely to go altogether unpunished."[51]

Everett was instructed to inform the foreign secretary that "if the facts turn out as stated, this Government thinks it a clear case for indemnification."[52] Webster also wanted to convey to the government in London a clear warning:

The United States and England, now by far the two greatest commercial nations in the world, touch each other both by sea and land at almost innumerable points, and with systems of general jurisprudence essentially alike, yet differing in the forms of their Government and in their laws respecting personal servitude; and that so widely does this last-mentioned difference extend its influence, that without the exercise to the fullest extent of the doctrine of non-interference and mutual abstinence from anything affecting each other's domestic regulations, the peace of the two countries, and therefore the peace of the world, always will be in danger.[53]

The concerns of the American government were eventually embodied, in near encyclopedic detail, in a formal protest from Mr. Everett to Lord Aberdeen on 1 March 1842.[54] It left the British authorities unmoved.[55] It would therefore fall to Lord Ashburton, in his special and wide-ranging diplomatic mission to the United States—examined in detail in chapter 3—to see if this impasse could be broken.

In the meantime, the 17 survivors of those who had risen up to seize the *Creole* in pursuit of freedom remained in custody in Nassau, and it was to this important matter that attention next turned. The procedure to be followed had been set out in the dispatch of Lord Stanley to Sir Francis Cockburn, dated January 31, in which he had transmitted the opinion of the imperial law officers.[56] In it, he instructed the governor to inform the US consul that it would be unlawful to surrender those in custody for trial in America and that they could not be prosecuted for murder or like offenses in the Bahamas. While the law officers had expressed the strong view that the facts of the incident would not sustain a charge of piracy, this was the only crime which could, in the circumstances, be judicially investigated. Should the US consul think it appropriate to prefer such a charge, Cockburn was to afford him "every facility" to do so. If not, Stanley concluded, "You will have no further duty to perform but you will leave them to obtain their discharge according to the regular course of law."[57]

Cockburn followed these instructions upon receipt by writing to the new US consul, Timothy Darling, on March 30.[58] It was only his second

day in the job. In his reply on the following day, Darling requested that
the prisoners be retained in custody to permit him time to communicate
with his government.[59] This the governor felt unable to do. Rather, he
would take steps to convene "a Special Session of the Admiralty Court to
enable you, should you decide on so doing, to bring forward the charge
of Piracy."[60] If so, the attorney general of the Bahamas would afford him
"every facility." That court, in turn, could consider any application for
delay.[61] In reply, the consul agreed to avail himself—though doubtless
reluctantly—of this opportunity and to accept the offer of the services
of the attorney general. He would, he wrote, then press upon its judges
"the urgent and absolute necessity existing that proper time should be
allowed for procuring the necessary witnesses in the case, that the ends
of justice be not defeated."[62] As Darling subsequently explained his actions to Secretary of State Webster, had he done otherwise: "The British Government might have said that these men escaped from justice in
consequence of the American Consul's refusal to prefer charges; and in
this case I might have exposed myself to censure from the Government
of the United States."[63]

In the course of the following days, Darling furnished the attorney
general with the depositions of the officers and crew of the *Creole* and
one of its passengers who, confusingly, had several variants to his name.
Kerr-Ritchie explained, "Joseph or Jacob Lietener or Leidner—spelled
variously in the documentation—was a Prussian who served as mate to
the steward in exchange for free passage to New Orleans."[64] In addition,
"[t]hree of the female Cabin passengers (still residing on the Island) who
were slaves on board the *Creole* were examined, but nothing material to
the charge [of piracy] was elicited from them."[65] This, he considered,
made it all the more important that the proceedings be delayed until
the next regular session of the court, which was due to take place on 28
June 1842.[66]

The Special Session convened on April 16. As Sir Francis Cockburn
was later to remark, the 17 "were brought into Court in custody of the
Provost Marshal upon which the Attorney General of this Colony moved
on behalf of the American Consul who was in Court at this time that they

. . . should be committed by the Court for trial for Piracy at the next General Session of the same Court, there not being evidence in the Colony to enable giving out a Bill of Indictment."[67] The court was presented with the depositions relating to the fact circumstances of the *Creole* incident, mentioned above, as well as a sworn statement by Darling concerning the steps that would be taken to secure, in a timely fashion, further evidence and witnesses from the United States.[68]

The judges then withdrew "for at least an hour" to consider the matters raised.[69] Upon their return, the Chief Justice, John Campbell Lees, verbally rendered the unanimous judgment of the court. It was no surprise, given what has been said above, that all 17 were ordered to be discharged. In doing so, the chief justice is said to have remarked: "It has pleased God to set you free from the bonds of slavery; may you hereafter live the lives of good and faithful subjects of Her Majesty's Government"[70] or words to like effect.[71]

The formal note of judgment, for long lost,[72] was shortly thereafter published in the *Royal Gazette*.[73] It is reproduced in full, for ease of reference, in appendix 2 of this study.[74] In an echo of the approach adopted by the law officers in London, the court first held that it lacked jurisdiction to inquire into an alleged murder by foreign nationals, committed on a foreign vessel, whilst on the high seas. Its jurisdiction in such extraterritorial circumstances extended solely to instances of piracy "for pirates, being deemed enemies of all mankind, could be tried by any nation having competent tribunals for the purpose." It then proceeded to set out its view of the constituent elements of that offense. In doing this, the judges made it clear that in this instance there had been, in the evidence before them, no piratical intent on the part of those who had been detained in custody. Their analysis contained the following, particularly explosive, *obiter dictum*, i.e., something said in passing:

> That nothing can be more clear than that the laws of one country or state cannot justly bind the subjects of another independent country or state, and that therefore if the subjects of the one are captured and held in bondage by the subjects of the other, such persons have a natural and

indefeasible right to recover their liberty when they have the power of
doing so. The slaves on board the Creole were thus situated, and could
only regain their liberty by taking temporary possession of the vessel, and
having so taken possession of her, it appears by facts which have come
to our knowledge, and by the examinations which have been taken, that
they intended to make no farther use of her than to convey themselves
to a British settlement to place themselves under the protection of the
British laws.

The attention of the court next turned to the request, made on behalf
of the American consul, that a postponement of the proceedings should
be ordered to permit further admissible evidence or testimony to be pro-
cured from the crew and passengers of the *Creole,* then in the United
States. This the court would have been minded to grant had the judges
"entertained any reasonable supposition that credible evidence could be
brought to convict the prisoners of piracy." They had "read attentively"
the depositions from the same individuals which had been submitted and
concluded, with reluctance, that they revealed no such prospect. The
application for postponement was consequently refused.[75]

In dealing with the text of the examination of Mr. Lightner—*semble*
Lietener or Leidner—which was the most relevant of those before it,
the judgment stated, in part, as follows: "The examinant was one who
signed the protest of the 7th of December last, at New Orleans, a protest
notorious to everyone in this community, for its gross mis-statements of
facts."[76] It should be noted in this regard that Darling, in his written report to Secretary of State Webster dated April 16—and thus based on his
recollection of what had transpired in court earlier the same day rather
than the subsequent written note of judgment—indicated that the chief
justice had gone further than this verbally. In his recollection, Chief Justice Lees had stated "that if all the persons who signed the Protest were
present to give their testimony, he should feel it to be his duty to charge
the jury not to believe them upon their oath."[77] Contemporaneous press
reports were to like effect.[78]

The available evidence suggests that Webster first saw the dispatch from Darling rather than the published note of judgment and was far from amused. On 4 May, Webster forwarded the former to Lord Ashburton, then in Washington, DC. Webster expressed the view that the doctrines "promulgated by the Chief Justice of that Colony are sufficiently startling."[79] Later the same month, he articulated his reaction to these developments, in greater detail, in a private letter (sent from Boston) to Edward Everett in London. He remarked:

> You will have seen what passed in the court at Nassau, when the consul of the United States made an attempt to bring the mutineers and murderers to trial as pirates. We have never said nor supposed they could be tried in the British courts as pirates; but the Chief Justice of the Bahama Islands completely justifies these persons for all they have done, and goes far out of his way to express doctrines and sentiments which appear to us absolutely ferocious. If such sentiments were to pervade British tribunals, and to find favour at home, consequences of the worst character must certainly ensue.[80]

The language of Chief Justice Lees was "as little capable of being misunderstood as it is of being justified or excused."[81]

The judicial outcome of the *Creole* affair in Nassau clearly presented as a further, and not insignificant, irritant to Anglo-American relations and, in its timing, posed an additional and unwanted element of complexity to the diplomatic efforts then underway to bring about an easing of tensions between the two countries. It is to those efforts that this study now turns.

Chapter 3

The *Creole* Incident in Anglo-American Diplomacy

THE WEBSTER–ASHBURTON NEGOTIATIONS

The arrival of the *Creole* in New Orleans in early December 1841 triggered heated debate in the United States.[1] For six weeks or more, public, political, and scholarly commentary was, of necessity, based on the partial and, as noted above, controversial rendition of the facts of the incident contained in the formal protest of the crew and passengers made in that city at that time.[2] On 19 January 1842, the body of relevant material was supplemented when the Tyler administration transmitted to the Senate the correspondence received from the US consulate in Nassau. In so doing, Secretary of State Webster explained that although "no application has been made . . . by the owners or underwriters, requesting the interference of this Government," he had been directed "to prepare a despatch for the American minister in London, which will be forwarded without unnecessary delay."[3]

This undertaking was satisfied when, on January 29, Webster addressed a detailed communication to Everett in the British capital on this "very serious occurrence."[4] This was subsequently communicated to the Senate where it was received "with great applause by the southern and slave holding interests."[5] It was also reproduced by the American press. Everett was instructed to "lose no time in calling Lord Aberdeen's attention to it in a general manner . . . with a distinct declaration that if the facts turn out as stated, this Government thinks it a clear case for indemnification."[6]

The American claim for "redress" was anchored in its understanding of "the laws and usages of nations." In Webster's view,

> it would seem to have been the plain and obvious duty of the authorities at Nassau, the port of a friendly Power, to assist the American Consul in putting an end to the captivity of the master and crew, restoring to them the control of the vessel, and enabling them to resume their voyage, and to take the mutineers and murderers to their own country to answer for their crimes before the proper tribunal. One cannot conceive how any other course could justly be adopted, or how the duties imposed by that part of the code regulating the intercourse of friendly States, which is generally called the Comity of Nations, could otherwise be fulfilled.[7]

Rather than act in conformity with this duty, the colonial authorities rendered no appropriate aid and assistance. Indeed, "they did actually interfere to set free the slaves, and to enable them to disperse themselves beyond the reach of the master of the vessel or their owners."[8] This conduct could not be justified on the basis of the abolition of slavery in the Bahamas and the other dominions of the British Crown: "No alteration of her own local laws can either increase or diminish, or any way affect, the duty of the English Government and its colonial authorities in such cases, as such duty exists according to the law, the comity, and the usages of nations."[9]

Two further points should be made about the thrust of this important communication to Everett at this stage. First, in essence, it sets out the basis for a state-to-state claim for "redress" or "indemnification." In other words, its focus was on compensation rather than restitution. Importantly, it contained no instructions to demand the return of the ringleaders of the revolt then held in Nassau jail.[10] Second, it emphasized the practical need to minimize the possibility of the recurrence of instances of this kind. In Webster's words:

The Bahamas (British possessions) push themselves near to the shores of the United States, and thus lie almost directly in the track of that great part of their coastwise traffic, which, doubling the Cape of Florida, connects the cities of the Atlantic with the ports and harbours on the Gulf of Mexico, and the great commercial emporium on the Mississippi. The seas in which these British possessions are situated, are seas of shallow water, full of reefs and bars, subject to violent action of the winds, and to the agitations caused by the Gulf Stream. They must always, therefore, be of dangerous navigation and accidents must be expected frequently to occur, such as will cause American vessels to be wrecked on British islands, or compel them to seek shelter in British ports. It is quite essential that the manner in which such vessels, their crews, and cargoes, in whatever such cargoes consist, are to be treated, in these cases of misfortune and distress, should be clearly and fully known.[11]

Everett was to take the opportunity to leave the United Kingdom government "with a full conviction of the dangerous importance to the peace of the two countries of occurrences of this kind, and the delicate nature of the questions to which they give rise."[12]

While instructing Everett to raise the *Creole* incident with the British foreign secretary, Webster identified a further possibility for addressing this dispute: "As Lord Ashburton may shortly be expected here, it may be better to enter fully into it with him, if his powers shall be broad enough to embrace it."[13] As is well known, throughout the 1830s, Anglo-American relations "steadily worsened."[14] The unsettled northeastern boundary between the United States and the relevant British possessions in what is now Canada was perhaps the most pressing irritant. The situation had been worsened by the *Caroline* incident of December 1837. As Greenwood has remarked, this "had its origins in a rebellion against British rule in Canada in 1837. A group of insurgents and their American supporters occupied Navy Island, a British possession on the river boundary between Canada and the United States. They used the steamer *Caroline* to transport men and munitions to the island, from which they planned to attack the Canadian mainland."[15] Faced with this threat, a

British force entered the United States on December 29, set the vessel alight, and sent it over Niagara Falls. Two persons were killed. The tensions concerning this matter had continued to simmer and had worsened somewhat in the course of 1841. There was much talk of the need for an initiative to address these and other outstanding issues thus to reset the relationship between the two countries.[16]

It is of relevance for our purposes to note that, in the summer of 1839, Webster, who was then a US senator for Massachusetts—having decided to set aside for the time being his personal presidential ambitions—set sail for an extended visit to England. While this sojourn had several purposes, one was to familiarize himself "with the details of the Maine—New Brunswick boundary dispute."[17] Among those closely associated with his time in London was Joshua Bates, the American-born partner in Baring Brothers,[18] the then preeminent financial house in the United Kingdom and one with close historical ties to the United States. Among his "new acquaintances [was] Alexander Baring, Lord Ashburton, who had only recently relinquished the active management of the banking house that bore his name."[19]

Late the following year, General William Henry Harrison secured an emphatic victory in the US presidential election over the incumbent Martin Van Buren. Harrison was inaugurated in early March 1841 and appointed Daniel Webster as his secretary of state. Within five weeks, however, Harrison had died—to be replaced, amid some controversy, by Vice-President John Tyler of Virginia. While the great majority of the Harrison Cabinet promptly resigned, Webster elected to serve the "accidental President" and remained in post.[20] Later that year, the winds of change also blew hard in London: "The Melbourne Cabinet, Palmerston included, resigned in 1841, with Peel returning to the Premiership and the well-disposed Lord Aberdeen to the Foreign Office."[21]

In these more propitious circumstances, the idea of a special mission charged with the resetting of the transatlantic relationship was quickly revived by the new British administration. Lord Aberdeen turned to Lord Ashburton to undertake this delicate and important task. He was regarded, for various reasons, as the "perfect choice."[22] Alexander Baring, the first Baron Ashburton, was a wealthy English financier who was well-connected on both sides of the Atlantic. Indeed, in his youth, he had spent over five years working in the United States. During this time, he met and married the elder daughter of the rich and influential US senator from Pennsylvania, William Bingham.[23] Furthermore, the Baring "family firm" had close and longstanding ties with Washington and had, for instance, played a significant role in arranging the financing for the Louisiana Purchase.[24] Finally, and importantly, Lord Ashburton was on friendly terms with Daniel Webster, the new and Anglophile secretary of state (see figs. 5 and 6).

It should be stressed that the decision to send Ashburton to Washington, DC, to undertake the delicate task of seeking to resolve a range of outstanding differences with the United States was wholly unrelated to the *Creole* incident. Indeed, he accepted the invitation to undertake this special mission[25] some five days before the first dispatch from Sir Francis Cockburn in Nassau outlining what had occurred arrived at the Colonial Office in London.[26]

The formal mandate to undertake these negotiations was to rest with Ashburton and not with the British minister in the American capital. As Aberdeen was to explain to Fox in a private note dated 3 January 1842: "I think you will be yourself aware of the improved prospect of success which such a mission must have, at the present moment, and especially when entrusted to such a man as Lord Ashburton. At the same time you will, I hope, rely on the sincerity of my declaration that your own conduct has given entire satisfaction."[27] In reply, the British envoy assured the Foreign Secretary of his desire to afford the special mission any assistance it might require. He added: "Nothing can possibly be better than the tone and temper in which Mr. Webster has received the announcement of Lord Ashburton's appointment."[28]

Given what has been said above, taken in conjunction with the slowness of transatlantic communication, it remained to be seen whether Webster's hope that Ashburton's instructions would be such as to encompass the *Creole* affair would be realized.[29] As Ashburton was determined to commence his mission at the earliest moment, these had to be prepared under considerable pressure of time.[30] Given the complexity of the subject matter, it is not surprising that there were to be several iterations of them. By way of illustration, a lengthy memorandum on the subject, dated February 8, addressed the northeastern boundary, the *Caroline* incident, the right of search at sea, and like matters but contained no reference to the *Creole*.[31] This is not particularly curious. While the British had for weeks been aware that the incident would be a source of friction with the United States, that trouble had not yet arrived; there had been no formal protest from the American mission in London, and the government may not even have been aware of the content of the January 29 dispatch from Webster to Everett outlining the approach the protest would take.[32]

The overall situation remained unchanged at the time of Ashburton's departure for the United States. On March 3, while his envoy was *en route,* the foreign secretary informed him, in a letter marked "Private," that his instructions had yet to be finalized but that he hoped to bring that matter to a conclusion in the near future. In the meantime, he was ordered "to abstain from anything like a final decision on the subject of the North East boundary. All other matters you may discuss freely and advance as rapidly as you please."[33]

There exists some ambiguity as to whether this freedom of maneuver extended to the issues surrounding the *Creole*. Aberdeen took the opportunity in the same dispatch to mention that a formal claim had just been delivered to the Foreign Office by Everett but that he had not yet had sight of the same. He clearly anticipated that it would have as its focus the fate of the ringleaders then still in Nassau jail awaiting news of their fate. In this context, he drew the attention of Lord Ashburton to the recent debate on this topic in the House of Lords, discussed in the previous chapter of this work, where all had agreed "that the trial, or delivery to the United States, of the accused, would be contrary to law. This unanimity precludes all possibility of doubt with respect to our conduct; but we must do the best that we can to put the matter on a right footing, and to obviate irritation and resentment."[34] Given this wording, Ashburton could well have considered it to constitute sufficient authority to address the matter in his forthcoming discussions with Webster and, as will be seen below, he proceeded to do so.[35]

Lord Aberdeen's prediction as to the thrust of the American claim proved to be erroneous. Dated 1 March 1842, Everett in his *demarche* followed the outline contained in his instructions from Webster of January 29 as summarized above.[36] It contained no explicit demand for the return of the surviving 17 mutineers then in Nassau jail. Rather he wove an even more detailed and complex legal, "moral," and political case for compensation and the need for appropriate guarantees as to future conduct.[37]

Ashburton arrived in Washington, DC—still without his final instructions—on 4 April 1842 and was granted an audience with President Tyler on the 6th. Webster, for his part, "received him, less as an envoy than as a friend."[38] It was within this positive context that he moved into his residence overlooking Lafayette Square (now known as Ashburton House) in view of the White House and within easy reach of the Department of State.[39] As Jervey and Huber have remarked, he "was soon engaged in informal discussions with Webster on various matters that they hoped would result in a treaty."[40] As will be seen in detail below, these intense negotiations would continue until early August.

While the settlement of the northeastern boundary was regarded by both countries as the ultimate prize and thus dominated the agenda, discussions on other matters were taken forward in parallel. As Adams reminds us, *Creole*-related issues came into focus at an early stage "since there was much public excitement about it, and Ashburton felt that it demanded consideration."[41] The initial exchanges between the two were promising. This was assisted in large measure by the disinclination of the United States to use this opportunity to press its case for reparations. Ashburton informed Aberdeen on April 25, "The arguments for compensation are not relied upon and will not be [pushed?]; and in conversation with me it was admitted by Mr Webster that they depend entirely upon the truth of the facts, viz—whether the authorities interfered to force the landing of the negroes."[42] While this international legal claim was not abandoned, it was in effect "parked" for present purposes. As will be seen in greater detail at a later stage of this study, it was to be revived and settled over a decade later.[43] Both agreed that the special mission afforded the opportunity to look to the future and seek to provide a degree of security against a repetition of the problems which had arisen.

From these early exchanges, two separate strands emerged. First, they sought a bilateral extradition agreement between the two states. As was seen in the previous chapter, the absence of such an agreement had loomed large in the consideration of the Law Officers of the Crown on whether the ringleaders of the *Creole* revolt could be returned to America to face trial. Second, there was a perceived need to explore options for securing some form of "prospective security" for navigation in the dangerous waters of the Bahamian archipelago.

However, even with the issue of compensation off the table, securing progress on these two distinct but interrelated elements proved to be far from straightforward. Several factors contributed to this. While Webster was to adopt a largely constructive attitude throughout,[44] Tyler's stance was more problematic: "The President, as a Virginian, has a strong opinion about the *Creole* case, and is not a little disposed to be obstinate on the subject."[45] A further irritant flowed from the slowness of communication with London and the inadequacy of Ashburton's instructions. In brief, official directions from London could never keep pace with the momentum of the dialogue in Washington. This was a constant source of frustration for Ashburton. This is well illustrated by an uncharacteristically curt and rather undiplomatic private letter sent to Aberdeen in late May. He complained to the Foreign Secretary that "I was, and still am, awaiting your instructions on important points"—extradition and security of the Bahama Channel among them.[46] In the circumstances, he had strayed somewhat beyond his mandate. He remarked, "[i]f I were master I would make a settlement of all these questions, and get up a [sound?] cordial feeling, but I know not what you may think of my projects."[47] "Unexpected" hindrances also manifested themselves from time to time.[48] One such came relatively early on and took the form of the receipt by Webster of the account prepared by the US consul in Nassau of the proceedings and outcome of the consideration of the *Creole* case in the Vice-Admiralty Court of the Bahamas. On May 4, the secretary of state forwarded to Ashburton these papers in which he characterized the views of the Chief Justice as "startling."[49] This did nothing to improve the atmosphere but would have been even worse had the papers been published by the American authorities. The views of the Bahamian chief justice on whether a slave could seek liberty through violence and on the trustworthiness of those who had signed the New Orleans Protest were, Ashburton informed Aberdeen, "precisely of a description to inflame one half of the population of this continent, and if it is our wish to live on terms of peace with them, our authorities should a little consider the value of a conciliatory spirit."[50]

Notwithstanding these difficulties, slow but incremental progress was recorded on both topics, and conclusions on them were arrived at in early August. It is to these outcomes that we now turn.

Extradition

It is indeed curious that in 1842 there should exist no formal arrangement between these two great powers regulating the surrender of fugitives from justice who had fled to, or otherwise located themselves in, the territory of the other. This basic form of international cooperation in criminal matters was well known in the community of nations and, fortunately, a direct precedent existed. The Jay Treaty of 1794 had contained a provision, though limited in scope, for this form of surrender between the two countries though it had since fallen into abeyance. In the intervening period, the British had "frequently but ineffectively" recommended that a new agreement be formulated.[51] The *Creole* incident had induced the Tyler Administration to show greater interest in this possibility.

Webster appears to have taken the early initiative on this topic and, in so doing, fully embraced that earlier precedent. Under its approach, extradition was available only with respect to those offenses specifically listed in the treaty. In 1794, this had been limited to murder and forgery. The central issue facing the negotiators in 1842 was, from the outset, the extent to which the list of enumerated crimes should be extended.

It should be noted at this stage that what was in contemplation was an arrangement between the United States and, in effect, the British Empire including, but not geographically limited to, the colony of the Bahamas. As Ashburton was to inform Aberdeen on April 25, "For the sake of our Canada frontier we should like to add arson: and America, to cover the Bahamas case."[52] He stressed his view that "there must be power to deliver mutineers, or we better make no treaty at all."[53]

It was agreed that the US secretary of state should prepare a draft text as the basis for discussion. This he did in short order, and Ashburton shared it with the foreign secretary on April 28.[54] While staying true to the form of the Jay Treaty, it suggested a significant extension of the list of crimes for which extradition would be available: viz, those charged "with the crime of murder, or piracy, or arson, or robbery, or forgery, or the utterance of forged paper, or with mutiny or revolt on board ship."[55] Ashburton reported to London that he believed the suggested list to go "much beyond" normal international treaty practice at that time. However, Webster had countered this by arguing that "the extension will be very acceptable on both sides on our Canada frontier."[56]

In his immediate response of May 26, the foreign secretary signaled the need to proceed with caution. He warned that "[t]he treaty of extradition of criminals may lead to some difficulty in defining the character of those acts which are committed by a slave in order to obtain his freedom. This will especially be the case on the High Sea, where no local jurisdiction exists."[57] Such questions would require careful and expert consideration. One week later, he wrote again raising further concerns over the inclusion of the "mutiny and revolt" at sea wording. In particular, he did not think "that our authorities would recognise" an attempt by slaves to recover their freedom "as mutiny or revolt."[58] He reminded Ashburton that the extradition provisions would require an enabling act of Parliament to enter into full force and effect and added, "I doubt much if with such a provision as this it would meet with the necessary assent of the two Houses."[59]

Ashburton, in response, accepted—though with evident reluctance—the conclusion of the foreign secretary. He admitted the "mutiny and revolt" provision, inspired by the *Creole* incident, "was in fact intended to cover precisely that which we cannot consent to cover."[60] Several alternative forms of wording had been canvassed and rejected in his discussions with Webster. However, he warned the foreign secretary of the need for some balance of conflicting interests and of the danger of taking the line of reasoning used to extremes: namely, that other crimes "might acquire an equivocal character from their being possibly connected with attempts of slaves to liberate themselves."[61] In this context, he specifically referenced murder which, in his view, "is more likely than any other crime to be connected with attempts at emancipation."[62] But, he insisted, without murder, "the highest of all crimes" there could be no meaningful extradition agreement. Finally, he urged Aberdeen to consider the positive impact of other protections for the individual contained in the wording of the clause.[63]

This was an undoubted setback to the ambitions of the negotiators on both sides. In a private letter to Everett in London, dated June 28, the US secretary of state made his views clear. He wrote, in part, as follows: "It is certainly not becoming between two nations, such as England and the United States, that one should make its territories an asylum for the perpetrators of any enormity of violence and blood, who may flee to it from the other. If this state of things continues, its continuance will not be our fault, nor its consequences, whatever they may be, chargeable to our account."[64]

Given what has been said above, it is somewhat surprising that the extradition provision, minus the wording on mutiny and revolt at sea,[65] was eventually accepted and found inclusion in the Webster–Ashburton Treaty[66] as Article X.[67] On 9 August 1842, the same day as the treaty was signed, Ashburton wrote to remind Webster that the extradition article "can have no legal effect within the dominions of Great Britain until confirmed by Act of Parliament."[68] This measure was duly enacted in August of the following year.[69] The Tyler Administration, for its part, stressed in its communication to the Senate the intended positive impact of those new arrangements on America's relationship with the British possessions in what is now Canada.[70] The list of offenses "is carefully confined to such offenses as all mankind agree to regard as heinous, and destructive of the security of life and property."[71] Great care had also been taken to exclude political offenses (such as treason) from its scope. Of rebellion and mutiny at sea, or the *Creole* incident in this context, there was no mention.

Security of the Bahama Channel

The second major strand of discussion relevant to the *Creole* to arise at an early stage concerned the need to explore the provision of greater security for American vessels transiting the hazardous waters of the Bahamian archipelago. Of special concern to Webster were those vessels with slaves on board forced by adverse weather, navigational misfortune, or violence to seek shelter or assistance in the ports or other internal waters of that British colonial possession. On 25 April 1842, Ashburton informed London of his support for providing some measure of security in this context, noting that "without it very irritating causes of dispute will be frequently recurring."[72] Perhaps more assuringly he noted, "With us our course seems clear, to hold fast to the principles of freedom in all our neighbouring Colonies but studiously to avoid tampering directly or indirectly with that state of things which a great adjoining independent state has thought proper to establish."[73]

As with the topic of extradition, it was agreed that the United States would take the lead by formulating its position in writing. This Webster promptly provided. It, as with extradition, took the form of a draft treaty clause (though it is clear that from the outset Ashburton thought this better done by way of revised instructions to the governor of the Bahamas).[74] The American draft was duly shared with Lord Aberdeen as an enclosure to a dispatch dated April 28.[75]

The draft clause was formulated in reciprocal terms and had as its geographic scope the relevant parts of the coasts of the United States and those of the contiguous island possessions of the British Crown. It was to apply to the merchant vessels of each party obliged "by stress of weather, shipwreck, or danger of enemies or pirates . . . driven to seek shelter in any of the ports of the other country, or . . . carried into the same by unlawful force, usurpation, or mutiny, or revolt of the persons on board." Vessels so situated would be entitled to security and protection while there, and to refit, repair and reprovision as necessary. They would be permitted to continue their voyage "without obstruction or interference of the local authorities and without inquiry into the character or condition of persons or things on board." In instances of mutiny or revolt "the owner or owners, or their agents, or the Consul of the country to which the vessel belongs, shall be properly aided in all lawful attempts to restore the authority of the master, and to enable said vessel to proceed on her voyage."

In his covering note, Ashburton stressed that the draft was being shared with the foreign secretary "more as explanatory of what America wants" than an indication of what had been (even tentatively) agreed. He wished to know how far he could go in his future discussions on this topic but stressed that he had "a strong opinion that something must be done, and is fairly done. I further believe that going as far as we can in this matter, will have generally a tendency to conciliate leading interests here."

Webster's proposal was not well received in London and, it is clear from the reply to Ashburton, that it was to be given no encouragement. Lord Aberdeen outlined his position thus:

> Touching the *Creole* affair, I very much fear it will be impossible to give any positive security against a repetition of the same kind of proceeding. This is quite clear, that whether driven by stress of weather or forcibly brought within British jurisdiction, the slaves must at once be free. In a British port, we could not place them at the mercy of the American Consul for an hour. If the Americans must send a slave cargo along the coast, why not give it convoy by one of their own vessels. We shall certainly do nothing to encourage mutiny either among slaves or freemen; but if the slaves bring a vessel into an English port, I do not see how we can again consign them to slavery, however we might be disposed to deal with them as mutineers.[76]

Sale of Estates, Pictures and Slaves in the Rotunda, New Orleans

FIG. 1. Slave Auction in the rotunda of the St. Louis Hotel, New Orleans. *Sale of Estates, Pictures, and Slaves in the Rotunda, New Orleans,* illustrated by W. H. Brooke FSA and engraved by J. M. Starling, in J. S. Buckingham's *The Slave States of America,* vol. 1 (Fisher, Son, & Co., 1842). CC BY 4.0.

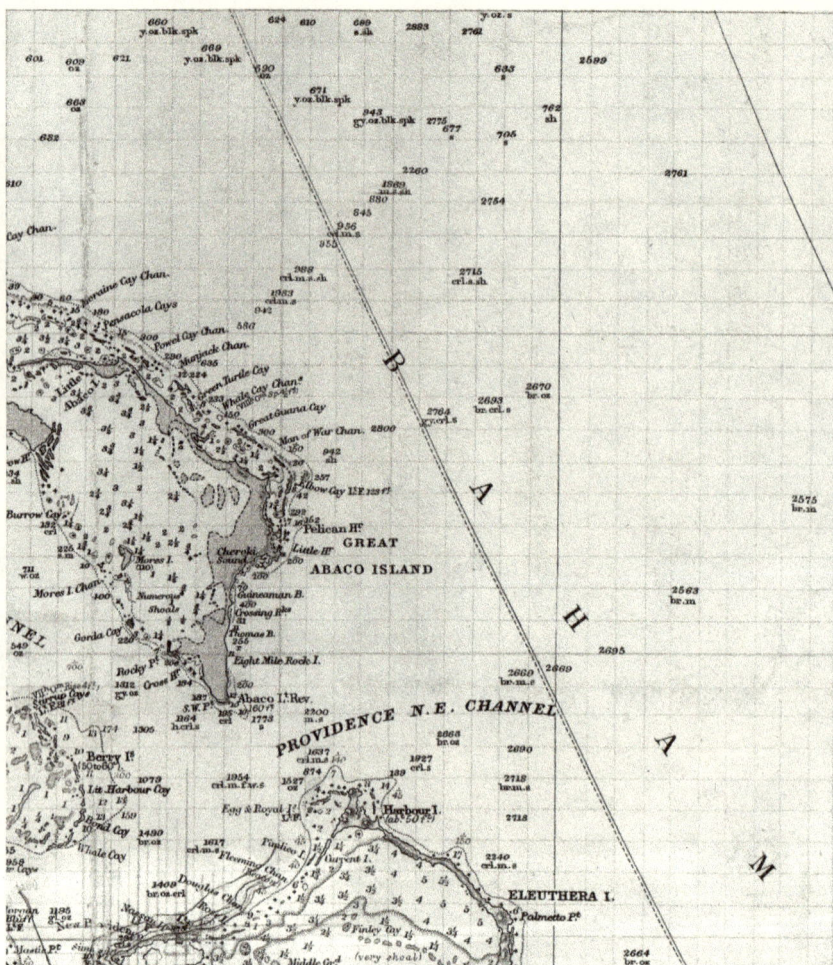

FIG. 2. Extract from a navigational chart showing Abaco and the surrounding area. Admiralty Chart, "West Indies Islands and Caribbean Sea," 1876. Extract reproduced courtesy of the National Library of Scotland.

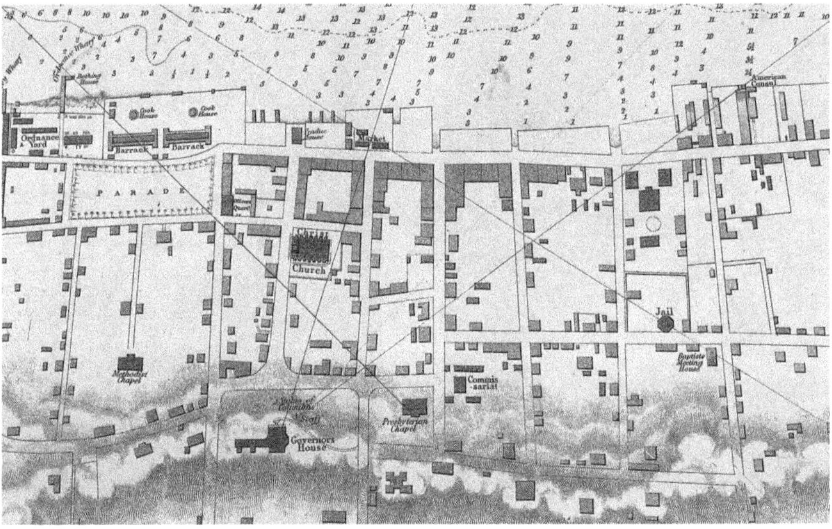

FIG. 3. Extract from a chart of Nassau Harbor showing the location of Government House, the office of the American consul, and other public buildings. Admiralty Chart, "West Indies: Nassau Harbour," 1841. Extract reproduced courtesy of the National Library of Scotland.

FIG. 4. Nassau Jail. Photograph by the author. The building now houses the Nassau Public Library.

FIG. 5. Portrait of Daniel Webster, painted in 1842 by George P. A. Healy. Reproduced courtesy of the New York Historical Society.

FIG. 6. Portrait of Alexander Baring, Lord Ashburton, painted in 1842 by George P. A. Healy. Reproduced courtesy of the New York Historical Society.

FIG. 7. Seal of the United States affixed to the Webster–Ashburton Treaty. Photograph by the author. The original is housed in the National Archives, London, FO 94/341.

FIG. 8. Portrait of Judah P. Benjamin, painted in 1853 by Adolph Rinck. Reproduced courtesy of the Louisiana Supreme Court Portrait Collection.

FIG. 9. Portrait of Justice Henry A. Bullard, painted in 1843 by Thomas C. Healy. Reproduced courtesy of the Louisiana Supreme Court Portrait Collection.

FIG. 10. Engraving of Frederick Douglass, ca. 1845. From the collection of the Library of Congress, Prints and Photographs Division.

Upon its receipt, Ashburton felt obliged to inform Webster that not only could the United Kingdom not accept his draft but that "the real difficulties attending the case did not at present permit us to see our way towards the proposal of any stipulations by treaty for this purpose."[77] The US secretary of state did not conceal his considerable disappointment at this development "as it left unsatisfied the President himself and a large party in Congress, connected with the interests of the South."[78] This was to the secretary of state not merely a political setback; there were also important issues of principle at stake. He confided to Everett in London in a private communication on June 26: "I deem it indispensable to the quieting of excited apprehensions, allaying resentments, and giving just security for the future, that some regular stipulations be entered into, or, at least, some authentic declaration given, that the British colonial authorities shall be made to respect the rules which usually regulate the intercourse of friendly states, their citizens, and subjects. No man can well doubt the necessity of this, who has taken notice of certain judicial proceedings in the Bahama Islands."[79]

The lead negotiators had a "long and desultory conversation"[80] as to the remaining options for treating the issue of preventative security as the treaty provision route had been blocked by London. Ashburton had considered leaving the matter entirely to one side thus allowing it to be subject to further exchanges through the normal course of transatlantic diplomacy. Such a stance might, however, serve to undermine his entire mission. As he noted in a dispatch to the foreign secretary, "I am here before the public, as a person to settle differences and difficulties, and . . . here this *Creole* case owing to the interests connected with it, is the chief of these difficulties."[81] He warned that "the ardour of the Government here towards these negotiations is cooled, since they find that their objects are not to be satisfied."[82]

Under the circumstances, the negotiators decided to explore addressing the topic through a formal exchange of letters. To this end, they rather hurriedly prepared rough drafts which could be sent to London for consideration. Those penned by Ashburton had three central elements: (a) an acknowledgement of the radically different approaches ad-

opted by the UK and US to the question of the enslavement of persons;
(b) an affirmation that through strictly confining the execution of those
laws "in our own dominions," they would "maintain in every respect
a reciprocity of good neighbourhood" and "continuously abstain from
any interference, directly or indirectly" with the clash of legal cultures
on this topic; and (c) an undertaking that the competent authorities in
the relevant British possessions would be "informed and instructed" to
comply with these principles and to refrain from any "provocation or
excitement, which they may be able legally to prevent."[83]

London having been so alerted, the negotiators turned their attention
to the refining of both the form and substance of the proposed exchange.
The latter proved to be far from straightforward and "at least a dozen
[revision?] attempts at explanation were tried."[84] These efforts stretched
right to the last moment as the convention was being readied for signa-
ture in early August. A final "querulous and foolish letter from the President" gave rise to a fear that the opportunity might be lost. Fortunately,
the terms of this partial "settlement on this point was at last but sulkily"
accepted by Tyler.[85]

It consisted of three parts. In the first, Webster set out, in considerable detail, the nature and extent of America's practical, policy, and legal
concerns surrounding the *Creole* incident and analogous cases brought
about by force of weather or navigational misfortune. It records the regret of the president that Ashburton was "not empowered" to enter into
a treaty stipulation for the "better security of the United States" in the
waters of the Bahamas in such circumstances.[86] Notwithstanding this
fact, it concluded with the hope (and expectation) that Ashburton "may
still be so far acquainted with the sentiments of your Government as to
be able to engage that instructions shall be given to the local authorities in
the islands, which shall lead them to regulate their conduct in conformity
with the rights of citizens of the United States, and the just expectations
of their Government, and in such manner as shall, in future, take away
all reasonable ground of complaint."[87]

The second element of the package took the form of Ashburton's
reply to the secretary of state.[88] In it, he acknowledges the importance of

the subject and explains that at the time of his departure for the United States, no formal protest over the *Creole* affair had been received by his government; it was not among the topics "which it was the immediate object of my mission to discuss."[89] Given the complexity and delicacy of the legal, policy, and practical issues to which it gave rise, he had concluded, with regret, that it would be better to be "treated in London, where it will have a much increased chance of settlement."[90] He was, however, prepared to provide the following assurance and explanation as to the future:

> I can engage that instructions shall be given to the Governors of Her Majesty's colonies on the southern borders of the United States to execute their own laws with careful attention to the wish of their own Government to maintain good neighbourhood, and that there shall be no officious interference with American vessels driven by accident or by violence into those ports. The laws and duties of hospitality shall be executed, and these seem neither to require nor to justify any further inquisition into the state of persons or things on board of vessels so situated, than may be indispensable to enforce the observance of the municipal law of the colony, and proper regulation of its harbors and waters.
>
> A strict and careful attention to these rules, applied in good faith to all transactions as they arise, will, I hope and believe, without any abandonment of great general principles, lead to the avoidance of any excitement or agitation on this very sensitive subject of slavery, and, consequently, of those irritating feelings which may have a tendency to bring into peril all the great interests connected with the maintenance of peace.[91]

In his reply—the third and final element of the approach adopted—Webster acknowledged that there "may be weight" in the reasons advanced to referring to London the consideration of such further stipulations as may prove necessary to remove all causes of complaint associated with this difficult topic.[92] The president placed "his reliance on those principles of public law which were stated in my note," and on "your lordship's engagement" in reply.[93]

Shortly thereafter, Ashburton wrote to the foreign secretary to inform him of how the *Creole* issue—"my great plague"—had finally been disposed of.[94] With evident reluctance, the president agreed: "How it may be considered by you remains to be seen."[95] In the event, his fears that it might be repudiated in London were not well-founded. That said, the commitments made were neither embraced by his government with enthusiasm nor implemented by it with promptitude. By way of illustration, in April of 1843, Viscount Palmerston asked the secretary of state for the colonies in Parliament what further instructions had been issued to relevant colonial governors pursuant to the above undertaking. In response, Lord Stanley stated that it had not been thought necessary "to issue any instructions subsequent to, or consequent on, that assurance."[96] As he explained, the governor of the Bahamas had been provided with the January 1842 opinion of the law officers (considered in chapter 2). He had then sought further instructions with respect to a number of hypothetical scenarios,[97] and this request had been responded to well in advance of the exchange of letters between Lord Ashburton and the US secretary of state. He had reason to believe that this communication to the governor—which was not in the public domain—was of such "a nature to comply with the request made on the part of Mr Webster, and the assurance which had been given."[98] The instructions in question were contained in the 30 April 1842 dispatch from the secretary of state for the colonies to Governor Cockburn, which is now available for consultation at the British National Archives at Kew in London.[99] The principal issue addressed was whether, in *Creole*-type circumstances, upon being informed that there were slaves on board an American merchant vessel desirous of securing their freedom, he as governor was bound to afford them protection against efforts designed to prevent them from so doing by coming on shore. In reply, Cockburn was instructed as follows: "Upon complaint being made to you on credible testimony persons were illegally detained against their will on board any vessel in a British Port, it would be your duty to verify the fact and to afford to persons so circumstanced the protection of British Law."[100] From what has been said above, it is to be very much doubted that this would have been seen by the Tyler administration as constituting the type of protection from "officious interference" which it thought it had secured from Lord Ashburton.

Fortunately, that question did not arise. Even without the complications it would no doubt have added, Ashburton had some concerns about how the deal struck on the issue of the *Creole* would be received by the US Senate, the advice and consent of which being required for the ratification of treaties. It should be noted that throughout the negotiations it was anticipated that two separate treaty instruments would emerge and require Senate consideration. One would settle and define the northeastern boundary and related matters. A separate and distinct treaty would treat extradition and provisions to strengthen the suppression of the African slave trade (a topic outside the scope of the present study). The *Creole* issues relating to greater security of navigation in Bahamian waters had been discussed under the umbrella of the negotiation of the latter, and it was expected that the exchange of letters would come before the Senate in that context.

On 9 August 1842, Ashburton wrote to Aberdeen informing him that he thought the boundary treaty was "quite safe" but that the fate of the other was "rather less certain."[101] In the final event, and at the urging of President Tyler,[102] it was agreed to consolidate the two texts.[103] This no doubt eased politically the eventual passage of this measure by the US Senate. Thus, the Webster–Ashburton Treaty, as it remains commonly known, was born (see fig. 7).

Chapter 4

Capitalism and Slavery
THE SLAVERS' QUEST FOR COMPENSATION

The Louisiana Insurance Cases

As noted previously, the *Creole* eventually docked in New Orleans in early December 1841, and this was swiftly followed by the formulation of the New Orleans Protest, duly sworn before a Notary Public on the 7th of that month by eight members of the ship's company and three of its passengers.[1] The protest was "against the winds and the waves, and the dangers of the seas generally, but more especially against the insurrection of the nineteen slaves . . . , and the illegal action of the British authorities at Nassau in regard to the remainder of the slaves on board said vessel, as the cause of all the loss and damage in the premises; and that no fault, negligence, or mismanagement, is, or ought to be, ascribed to these said appearers, or to any part of said brig's company."[2] The making of protests of this kind was "common practice"[3] designed, *inter alia,* to construct a degree of protection from legal liability. As has been pointed out elsewhere, "this is altogether an *ex parte* statement, and of course is the strongest case that can be made against the British authorities at Nassau, and in favour of those concerned in interest in the rescued slaves."[4] Its contents were particularly controversial in British circles; the Chief

Justice of the Bahamas opining that it contained "gross mis-statements of facts."[5] Fox, the British minister in Washington, was to inform the Foreign Secretary that it apparently contained "much falsehood and exaggeration," but reminded him that it was "principally directed" at the American insurance companies "in order to show that the officers and crew did all that depended upon them to prevent the loss of the so called property, by the liberation of the negroes."[6]

By 1841, marine insurance was a particularly well-established and relatively mature branch of commercial law in the United States. Levy reminds us, "In North America, the great colonial merchants were the first men to commodify perils into financial 'risks'—or 'risques,' as they were known in the seventeenth and eighteenth centuries. Through marine insurance they purchased from one another financial compensation in the event that their property was lost to a 'peril of the seas,' or an 'act of God.' A storm destroyed a vessel, a ship was seized by pirates—the merchant-insurance provided the merchant-owner compensation for the lost value of his cargo. To cope with the perils of seaborne trade, the insurance principle was born."[7] Unsurprisingly, "operators in the interstate slave trade often insured their shipments."[8] Those with a financial interest in the human "cargo" aboard the *Creole* were no exceptions. Upon its arrival in New Orleans, they called on their insurers to indemnify them against the losses sustained. They, in turn, denied liability. It was to prove to be a red-letter day for the Louisiana legal profession.

In total, some seven separate actions involving four different insurance companies made their way to and through the courts of that state arising out of the *Creole* mutiny.[9] Of those the best known is *McCargo* v. *New Orleans Insurance Company*. This insurer, established in 1805,[10] "was located in the heart of New Orleans 'Exchange Alley,' two blocks away from the city's slave pens."[11] Thomas McCargo had entered into an insurance contract with this company regarding twenty-six slaves shipped on the *Creole* and valued at $800 each. Separately the same slaver took out a policy with the Merchants' Insurance Company of New Orleans with respect to nineteen enslaved persons shipped on the *Creole* on the same voyage.[12] Though the policies in question had many similarities, there were differences which would prove to be material. Indeed, in the ensuing litigation of these two cases can be found the essence of the outcome of the wider consideration of the insurance aspects arising from the *Creole* mutiny before the courts of Louisiana.

In both cases, McCargo called for the insurers to indemnify him against loss. In each, liability was denied and the resulting disputes arose for separate judicial consideration in the Commercial Court. In the *New Orleans Insurance Company* case, a judgment was issued in favor of McCargo for $18,400.[13] As has been noted elsewhere, "the amount sued for was $20,800. The jury deducted $800 for one of the slaves who reached New Orleans in safety. A further sum of $1,600 appears to have been deducted, as half of the value of four of plaintiff's slaves, who were proved to have taken part in the insurrection, the jury being of opinion that their loss should be divided between the insurers and the plaintiff."[14] In the action against the Merchants' Insurance Company at first instance, McCargo also secured judgment in his favor. He was awarded $14,400—"a deduction of $800 having been made for one of the slaves who had reached New Orleans on the brig."[15]

The insurance companies appealed. For this purpose, each retained the same high-powered team of lawyers to represent them. It consisted of Judah P. Benjamin, the youthful rising star of the Louisiana legal profession in matters commercial (who was both a slave owner and member of the plantocracy),[16] his friend, and co-author of a legal text,[17] Thomas Slidell, and one F. B. Conrad. This did not mark the end of the involvement of this threesome in the *Creole* litigation appearing as they did for the insurers in *Lockett* v. *Merchants' Insurance Company of New Orleans*.[18]

McCargo v. *New Orleans Insurance Company* was "elaborately argued by brief and *viva voce*"[19] in the summer of 1844, and judgment was delivered by Justice Henry A. Bullard of the state supreme court in March 1845. As the judge noted, several actions had been raised against various New Orleans insurers: "As all the cases relate to the same voyage, and all the slaves insured were lost at the same time and by the same disaster, they have all been considered together; and it is supposed that the opinion which we are about to pronounce in one of the cases, will be decisive for all."[20]

The arguments presented by Benjamin and his co-counsel were both wide-ranging and scholarly. They covered several critical issues of insurance law as well as the domestic and international law relating to slavery and various relevant doctrines of the international law of the sea.[21] The arguments are replete not only with references to the Civil Code of Louisiana, to statute and case law, but also to doctrines of Roman law and to French, Spanish, and other authorities. Benjamin's treatment of slavery issues was regarded as unusually frank and sensitive by the standards of the day; in Levy's words, the approach adopted was "remarkably heretical."[22] By way of illustration, one of the lines of argument pressed by counsel for the insurers was that they had been, in law, discharged, the vessel having been rendered unseaworthy by virtue, *inter alia,* of overcrowding.[23] There being no federal legislation directly applicable to slave cargo, the point was argued by analogy from an act of Congress in 1819 regulating the matter of "ordinary passengers." Had it applied, the maximum number would have been 63. In the case of the *Creole,* at least 135 slaves had been embarked. The argument was advanced: "Now this Act of Congress was based upon considerations of humanity, and it was deemed necessary to enact such a law, although our country has always been disposed to encourage the immigration of foreigners. Will this court be disposed to recognize one standard of humanity for the white man, and another for the negro? Will any reasonable man say that 135 negroes would be as cheerful, contented and indisposed to insurrection, under such circumstances of discomfort, as they would have been in a larger and more commodious vessel?"[24]

At a later stage and on a different head of argument, it was directly put to the court "that slavery is a contravention of the law of nature, is established by the concurrent authority of writers on national law, and of adjudications of courts, from the era of Justinian to the present day."[25] In the course of addressing the nature of the responsibility of the Bahamian colonial authorities, counsel urged the following view of international law:

[D]oes the law of nations make it the duty of Great Britain to refuse a refuge in her dominions to fugitives from this country, whether black or white, free or slaves? It would require great hardihood to maintain the affirmative as to whites, but the color of the fugitive can make no possible difference. It will scarcely be pretended that the presumption of our municipal law that blacks are slaves, is to be made a rule of the law of nations; and, if not, in what manner are the British authorities to determine between the blacks and whites reaching their ports on the same vessel, the former asserting their liberty, and the latter denying the fact, and claiming the blacks as slaves?[26]

These and other kindred lines of argument advanced on behalf of the insurers were by no means commonplace in Louisiana or the Deep South in the 1840s. It is not surprising, therefore, though it is deeply ironic that Butler informs us that Benjamin's brief "was printed in pamphlet form and widely circulated" (see fig. 8).[27]

The terms of the policy in question exempted the insurers from "any liability on account of losses which might be sustained in consequence of a mutiny, or insurrection on board; they assuming all other risks, and particularly restraints, arrests, and detentions by foreign powers, or the emancipation of the slaves by foreign interference."[28] Not all of the *Creole*-related insurance policies were so broad in scope. In particular, in two instances the insurance companies were not specifically exempted from loss flowing from mutiny or insurrection.[29]

To Justice Bullard, an experienced judge and well-respected Harvard graduate,[30] the "great question" of law which fell to be determined in *McCargo* v. *New Orleans Insurance Company*, and in other suits in which the insurers had excluded liability for insurrection or mutiny, was "whether the loss of the slaves was caused by the insurrection, or by illegal and unauthorized intervention on the part of the authorities of Nassau."[31] Before turning to the events in Nassau Harbor, the judge addressed several issues in brief. First, he concluded that the mutiny on the high seas had been "completely successful; all resistance was in vain, and no attempt was made by the whites to regain their ascendancy."[32] It was in this situation that the *Creole* entered British colonial internal waters. Second, notwithstanding this fact it was Bullard's view that the enslaved did not thereby, either *de facto* or *de jure,* become free: "We regard them still as slaves while on board, though in a state of insurrection. They had not ceased to be the property of their masters, although that right of property could not have been asserted in a British court, nor enjoyed within the exclusive influence of British law."[33] Finally, for present purposes, he accepted—as had the judge in the commercial court—that the letter from Webster to Ashburton of 1 August 1842, examined in chapter 3 above and in which he set out the American view of the distress rule in the international law of the sea, was "a true exposition of the law of nations on this subject."[34]

From this base, Bullard proceeded to examine, in fine detail, the facts as they related to the events concerning the *Creole* when in Nassau Harbor. As Johnson reminds us, the written record was now voluminous, including accounts retold several times over the years by key participants.[35] In so doing, the judge paid particular attention and gave special weight to the written correspondence between the representatives of the two states and especially the exchanges between the US consul and the governor of the Bahamas.[36] These were deemed to "afford much more satisfactory evidence of the true character of such transactions, than the statements even of the actors themselves, made afterwards from memory."[37]

Having completed his analysis of the official written correspondence of that period, Bullard next turned to the "parol evidence touching what occurred on the 12th of November, when the guard was withdrawn and the slaves left the vessel."[38] That evidence base was found to be "discordant and contradictory,"[39] manifesting a disconnect between the American and Bahamian witnesses.[40] Notwithstanding this divergence of recollection, some matters were clear to the court:

> 1st. That no violence was used on the occasion [12 November], and that not a single person from on shore, or the surrounding boats, boarded or attempted to board the Creole. 2d. That the four who voluntarily remained, were not disturbed, nor interfered with. 3d. That neither the

mate Gifford, not Merritt, gave any orders to the slaves to go below, or to remain on board when the guard should be withdrawn, nor exerted any authority to prevent the slaves from going on shore when the guard was withdrawn. 4th. That only nineteen were taken on shore by the British guard, with the consent of all concerned.[41]

From this examination of the evidence as to the facts, the judge moved to consider the crucial legal issue before him—namely, what, in the domestic law of insurance, was the true and efficient cause of the loss occasioned by the emancipation of the *Creole* slaves? The position in public international law was not the proper concern of the court but a separate matter for the two governments.[42] Bullard explained, "When several successive perils have been encountered, and a loss ensues, it is often difficult to determine which is, legally speaking, the true cause. The rule, *causa proxima, non remota spectatur,* is well established; but the *last,* is not necessarily the *proximate* cause."[43] It was in this context that Bullard considered the argument advanced on behalf of McCargo that, had the colonial authorities not thwarted it, the plot of the US consul with the aid of Captain Woodside and other American citizens might have been sufficient to recover control of the vessel and the enslaved persons on board thus obviating any loss. For Bullard, this was a pivotal issue for he had concluded that "[u]p to that moment no complaint had been made of improper interference on the part of the local authorities. That interference, such as it was, had been sought by the consul, and the mate of the brig."[44] The general principle that consent negates the possibility of legal wrong was thus acknowledged.

For the relevant facts, the court relied upon those contained in the New Orleans protest of 7 December 1841.[45] It was unconvinced. Bullard concluded that "neither the failure to purchase arms on shore, nor to rescue the *Creole* from the guard before the examination had been terminated can be imputed to the authorities of the island as a cause of the loss of the slaves."[46] Rather pointedly the court remarked that it might well be argued that the officer commanding the troops on board had a right to forbid the plotters from boarding the vessel and that "[i]t would hardly have comported with the good faith to have made an attempt at that time, by force of arms, to rescue the brig from the guard."[47]

On the basis of the above reasoning, it was held "that the insurrection of the slaves was the cause of breaking up the voyage, and prevented that part of the cargo, which consisted of slaves, from reaching the port of New Orleans; and, consequently, that the defendants are not liable on the policy in this case."[48] The judgment of the commercial court was reversed: "Ours is for the defendants, with costs in both courts."[49] This finding, in turn, had serious implications for the outcome of the litigation in which the relevant policy had not specifically excluded the insurers from liability for mutiny or insurrection. One such was *McCargo* v. *Merchants' Insurance Company of New Orleans*. In this regard, the commercial court had held that "we have adopted the English law, according to which an insurance on slaves protects the assured against loss arising from mutiny and insurrection, unless that peril be expressly warranted against."[50] On appeal to the Louisiana Supreme Court, that earlier conclusion as to the law was affirmed. As "the loss was occasioned by the insurrection which, according to the policy was a risk assumed by the defendants . . . the plaintiff is entitled to recover."[51] McCargo's quest for financial recompense through the courts of Louisiana thus recorded a partial success. That said, in the majority of the *Creole* cases, the slavers were left empty-handed. They were not alone in feeling acute disappointment. As has been noted elsewhere, "proslavery ideologues howled in the southern press that Benjamin and Bullard had sided with the 'misguided fanatics' of the North who would abolish the 'rational freedom' of slavery."[52]

International Arbitration

The conclusion of the Louisiana litigation concerning marine insurance did not, however, mark the end of the quest by the slave "owners" disappointed by the outcome for reparation for the loss of their "property." While they had exhausted their domestic legal remedies in the United States, their focus turned once again to the issue of what redress, if any, they could obtain from the United Kingdom through the good offices of the American federal government. In this they were joined by the insurance companies which, in a minority of instances, had been obliged by the courts to compensate the slavers—on the basis that in so doing they had, in effect, inherited such claims for injury at the international level. This eventuality had been foreseen by Bullard in *McCargo v. New Orleans Insurance Company*. In his words, "It is not for us to decide, whether the conduct of the local authorities of Nassau in relation to the Creole, was such a violation of international comity, as to give just cause of complaint in the diplomatic relations of the United States with Great Britain. With the case, in that respect, we have nothing to do. Whether the loss shall fall upon the owners or the underwriters, the question of redress between the two governments remains the same."[53]

As previously discussed, from an early stage, the United States had protested at the actions of the British colonial authorities in Nassau and had demanded compensation for the freeing of the enslaved persons aboard the *Creole* in a manner which, in its view, constituted a violation of international law.[54] Though the intensity of the resulting diplomatic exchanges in this matter diminished following the conclusion of the Webster–Ashburton Treaty in 1842, this state-to-state claim remained unresolved. Nor did the *Creole* incident stand alone as an irritant to Anglo-American relations. As the president was to remind the US Senate in 1856, there was a "class of cases where the governments were directly at issue on grave questions of international law, that had caused much irritation between the two countries. These cases had been the subject of laborious investigation and frequent discussion in Congress and had been argued with eminent ability . . . until all hope of a settlement of them in the ordinary mode had been abandoned."[55]

In the absence of a "World Court," an institution which would have to await the post-World War I peace settlement for its imperfect creation,[56] one option was to establish, on an *ad hoc* basis, an arbitral body of some type to arrive at a final determination. Merrills and De Brabandere remarked:

One possibility is to set up a commission consisting of equal numbers of national arbitrators, appointed by the parties, and a neutral member (or umpire) to whom cases are referred if the national members cannot agree. The origins of this form of tribunal, frequently used to deal with claims arising out of injury to aliens, can be traced back almost 200 years. In the Treaty of Ghent (1814), the United States and the United Kingdom agreed that certain disputes between them should be arbitrated by national commissioners with reference to a disinterested third party in the event of disagreement.[57]

In the early 1850s, the two governments agreed to follow this earlier precedent and to create a further mixed-claims commission; a decision formalized by treaty on 8 February 1853 and ratified in July of the same year.[58] Its jurisdictional scope was extensive. By virtue of Article I, all unsettled claims "on the part of corporations, companies, or private individuals" which had been presented to and adopted by either government in respect of the other since the 1814 Treaty of Ghent fell within its remit. Each resulting determination was to be regarded as "a full, perfect and final settlement" of the claim in question.[59] On this basis, more than 100 claims involving a total value of several millions of dollars arose for consideration[60] within a tight and ambitious time frame.[61] The commission sat in London and commenced its work on 15 September 1853.

The US Supreme Court recalled in 1858, "This convention provided for the appointment of a board of commissioners, one to be named by each Government, and the two to appoint an umpire, to decide upon all claims in which a difference of opinion should occur."[62] The cases in question were presented for consideration not by the individuals or corporations in question but by agents appointed by the respective governments[63] thus underlining the interstate nature of the process.

The two states appointed fairly distinguished lawyers as their commissioners. In the case of the United States, Nathaniel G. Upham (1801–1869) was selected to undertake this task. He brought to the process some ten years of experience as an Associate Justice of the New

Hampshire Supreme Court. The British appointed Edmund G. Hornby (1825–1896), an up-and-coming member of the English Bar who would go on to enjoy a rather exotic judicial career as the chief judge of both the Supreme British Consular Court in Constantinople (1857–1865) and the British Supreme Court for China and Japan (1865–1876).[64] Pursuant to Article I of the treaty, both were required to solemnly declare "that they will impartially and carefully examine and decide, to the best of their judgment, and according to justice and equity, without fear, favour, or affection to their own country, upon all such claims as shall be laid before them."

As noted above, the treaty envisaged the appointment by the commissioners of "some third person to act as an arbitrator or umpire in any case or cases on which they may themselves differ in opinion";[65] said person was to "make and subscribe a solemn declaration, in a form similar to that which shall already have been made and subscribed by the Commissioners."[66] So central was the umpire to the architecture of this dispute settlement process that the appointment had to be made "before proceeding to any other business."

Agreement on this important matter did not prove straightforward. It was first discussed on 15 September 1853 where "[t]he names of several gentlemen were mentioned on either side, and the subject was deferred for further consideration."[67] Consensus on this point was eventually reached on October 12 when it was determined that Martin Van Buren (1782–1862), then in Florence, be approached and the offer of appointment was communicated to him the following day.[68] In it, the commissioners remarked, "In endeavouring . . . to fix upon an individual who should unite in himself the requisites of high character, exalted position and strict impartiality, they have experienced the greatest difficulty; nevertheless, they are happy to say they have been able to unite cordially in agreeing upon yourself and believe your appointment will be highly acceptable to their respective peoples and governments."[69] In making this approach, the commissioners had set their sights high. Van Buren, it will be recalled, was not only a distinguished lawyer, diplomat, and statesman but had also served as the eighth president of the United States (March

1837–March 1841).[70] It is a testament to his standing that an individual so fully associated with but one of the parties to the treaty of 1853 should prove acceptable to both.[71]

Inspired though this choice may have appeared, it was not to be. On October 22, the former president replied to the commissioners in the negative. In so doing, he remarked:

> No one can appreciate more highly than I do the importance, not to themselves only, but to the world, of the maintenance of friendly relations between our respective countries; and a satisfactory execution of this convention cannot fail to exert a most salutary influence in that direction. In view of motives so impressive, I do most sincerely regret to find myself constrained, by considerations which I dare not disregard, to decline the appointment you have done me the honor to make. After spending the principal part of my life in the public service, I have for several years withdrawn myself not only from all personal participation in public affairs, but from attention to business of every description, save only what has been indispensable to the management of my private affairs.[72]

This communication was received by the commissioners on October 28.[73] It placed them in a position of some difficulty as their formal work could not commence until this post was filled and the activities of the commission, as noted above, were time-limited. Thus, only three days later, commissioner Upham suggested to his British counterpart the appointment of Joshua Bates as umpire.[74] This was, in some respects, a surprising development. Unlike Van Buren, Bates had no experience in diplomacy and had never held a high public office. Rather, he was a wealthy banker—a senior partner in Baring Brothers.[75] He did, however, possess a number of attractive characteristics. As Upham explained, "Mr Bates is an American-born citizen, who in early life gained such reputation for intelligence, energy, honorable character, and business acquirements, as to cause a demand for his services in the leading banking house of this country and the world. His long residence in England in that position and his great success has established him here permanently as his adopted home, and has given him a standing and character that should impart full confidence to the claimants of both countries, as well as to the governments themselves, in the intelligence, integrity, and impartiality of his decisions."[76] Hornby promptly agreed[77] and Bates, who was London-based, was offered and quickly accepted this crucial appointment.[78]

In their November 1 letter offering Bates the post of umpire, the commissioners informed him that, in their view, he possessed "in a high degree the essential qualities of an umpire, namely, high character, and freedom from all personal and national bias."[79] It may seem curious to some that, for a role which would involve detailed consideration of complex issues of public international law, no mention was made of this factor; more curious still, unlike Van Buren, Bates had no prior legal training.[80] This may be explained, at least in part, by the terms of Article I of the treaty. As noted above, this required the commissioners and the umpire to act with impartiality and to decide the cases before them "*according to justice and equity*" rather than on the basis of the Law of Nations alone. In effect, this enabled the umpire to make determinations *ex aequo et bono*. As has been pointed out elsewhere, "the ancient concept of *ex aequo et bono* is based upon the idea of 'fundamental fairness' as a guideline principle in *arbitration* and other dispute settlement processes. Provided that the parties expressly agree, it enables judges and arbitrators to decide a case according to what—in literal translation of the original Latin phrase—'is fair (or equitable) and good' . . . That is also to say 'in good conscience' and notwithstanding the written law."[81]

It was within this rather unusual institutional context that the dispute between the United States and Great Britain concerning the *Creole* incident of 1841 eventually arose for determination. The case was presented in March 1854 and heard in June. The commissioners, as will be seen in detail below, formally concluded that they were unable to agree on September 26.[82] Under the circumstances, the *Creole* case, among others, was "then ordered to be committed to the decision of the umpire."[83] It should be noted that the American Commissioner did not formulate a separate judgment in the *Creole* case as he considered that "the judgment delivered by him in the case of the 'Enterprize' was equally applicable."[84] It is to his analysis in that case that we must therefore now turn.

The *Enterprize* Award of 23 December 1854

In late January 1835, the brig *Enterprize,* an American merchantman, set sail from Alexandria, then part of the District of Columbia, for Charleston, South Carolina. It had on board in excess of 70 enslaved persons, and the voyage was considered lawful under US coastal slave-trading statutes. Whilst at sea, it encountered adverse weather conditions and was driven off course. In the words of Umpire Bates, "after encountering head winds and gales, and finding their provisions and water running short, it was deemed best by the master to put into Hamilton, in the island of Bermuda, for supplies."[85] It arrived there on February 11. The opportunity was also taken to undertake some repairs to the vessel's sails.[86] Bermuda was then, and remains, a British possession and, as such, was a territory to which the 1833 statute giving effect to the abolition of slavery applied.

During its stay in port for reprovisioning and repair, "no one from the shore was allowed to communicate with the slaves."[87] Notwithstanding this fact, before the *Enterprize* could depart, a writ of *habeas corpus* was served upon the captain. As the British commissioner was to note, "this was obtained, at the instance of an association of free blacks in the island . . . requiring his appearance before the court, and the production of the slaves still remaining on board. Upon the argument of the case, the court declared that there was no law authorizing the detention of the slaves, and they were accordingly set at liberty."[88] Six of the enslaved opted to decline to take advantage of this proclamation and returned to the vessel which then departed British waters.[89]

It was on the basis of the above facts that the United States submitted its claim for compensation on behalf of the slave "owners" concerned. In the view of Thomas, the American agent and counsel before the commission, the "owners" had been deprived of their "property" in violation of the Law of Nations.[90] Compensation for the resulting financial loss was the necessary consequence. Upham, the United States commissioner, agreed. In his opinion, the principles of international law applicable to cases of this type were as follows:

I. That each country is entitled to the free and absolute right to navigate the ocean, as the common highway of nations; and, while in the enjoyment of this right, retains over its vessels the exclusive jurisdiction of its own laws.

II. That a vessel compelled by stress of weather or other unavoidable necessity, has a right to seek shelter in any harbor, *as incident to her right to navigate the ocean,* until the danger is past and she can proceed again in safety.

III. That *the enjoyment of such shelter,* being *incident to the right to navigate the ocean,* carries with it *the rights of the ocean,* so far as to retain over the vessel, cargo, and persons on board, the jurisdiction of the laws of her country.

IV. That the act of *3 & 4 Wm IV, ch. 73,* abolishing slavery in Great Britain and her dominions, could not overrule the rights of nations as laid down in these propositions.[91]

Having elaborated on each of these principles, in turn, the American commissioner concluded that "the Enterprize was entitled, under the immediate perils of her condition, to refuge in the Bermudas; that she had a right to remain there a sufficient time to accomplish the purposes of her entry, and to depart as she came; that the local authorities could not legally enter on board of her for the purpose of interfering with the condition of persons or things as established by the laws of her country; and that such an exercise of authority over the commerce and institutions of a friendly state is not warranted by the law of nations."[92]

Hornby, the British commissioner, did not take issue with the entirety of the analysis of his US colleague. For instance, he did not challenge the principle of exclusive flag state jurisdiction on the high seas. Indeed, Hornby accepted that significant limitations were imposed on a port state when foreign vessels sought shelter in instances of genuine distress. In his words, "it is undoubtedly true, as a general proposition, that a vessel driven by a stress of weather into a foreign port is not subject to the application of the local laws, so as to render the vessel liable to penalties which would be incurred by having voluntarily come within the local jurisdiction. The reason of this rule is obvious. It would be a manifest injustice to punish foreigners for a breach of certain local laws, unintentionally committed by them, and by reason of circumstances over which they had no control."[93]

In the view of the British commissioner, however, this rule, and the protection it afforded, did not apply in the fact circumstances of this case. Two primary arguments were advanced in this regard. The first was, in essence, that the concept of distress was not self-defining; a threshold of seriousness had to be satisfied in order to trigger the operation of the rule.[94] In his opinion, it had to be shown that "the Enterprize was compelled by *necessity* to put into the port of Bermuda."[95] This basic case had not been made out: "It is not pretended that the Enterprize was forced by storm into Bermuda. All that is asserted is, that her provisions ran short by reason of her having been driven out of her course. No case of pressing, overwhelming need is shown to have existed."[96] The mere avoidance of "the inconvenience of short rations" did not meet the threshold for triggering the operation of the international law rule.[97]

The second major line of argument advanced by the UK and embraced by Commissioner Hornby was that the distress rule was not an absolute one; it was subject to exceptions and such an exception applied in this instance. In the view of the commissioner under the distress rule, "while the vessel is . . . free from the operation of the local laws, it by no means follows that it is entitled to absolute exemption from the local jurisdiction; as, for example, it can scarcely be contended that persons on board the vessel would not be subject to the local jurisdiction for crimes committed within it."[98] A merchantman entering a foreign port in distress—properly so called—"brings with her (by the law of nations) immunity from the operation of the local laws for some purposes, but not for all, and the extent of that immunity is the proper subject of investigation and adjudication by the local tribunals."[99] The fundamental principle which should guide such a determination was that no port state can be called upon "to permit the operation of foreign laws within its territory when those laws are contrary to its interests or its moral sentiments."[100] Slavery was, he insisted, one such instance.

These arguments did not fare well in the award of the umpire delivered in late December 1854.[101] First, in an *ex cathedra* pronouncement, unencumbered by reasoning or reference to authority, Bates declared that the *Enterprize* had "entered the port of Hamilton in distress for provisions and water."[102] Second, the umpire concluded that the *Enterprize* was fully entitled to the protection of that rule. While slavery was "contrary to the principles of justice and humanity," it was not "contrary to the law of nations."[103] Consequently, the vessel "was as much entitled to protection as though her cargo consisted of any other description of property."[104] Thus, he concluded, "The conduct of the authorities at Bermuda, was a violation of the laws of nations, and of those laws of hospitality which should prompt every nation to afford protection and succor to the vessels of a friendly neighbor that may enter their ports in distress."[105] The claim of the United States was in this manner comprehensively upheld and compensation of $49,000 was ordered to be paid to the insurers of the slaves whose liberty had been secured in that British possession.[106]

The *Creole* Award of 9 January 1855

So broad in scope had been the judgment of the American Commissioner in the case of the *Enterprize* that he elected to rely upon it in relation to the two remaining claims which raised similar issues; namely, the *Creole* incident and the October 1840 wreck of the *Hermosa*, with 38 enslaved persons aboard, off the same Bahamian island of Abaco.[107] As Edmund Hornby was later to note, Mr. Upham "did not deliver any judgment in these cases, as he considered that the judgment delivered by him in the case of the 'Enterprize' was equally applicable."[108]

The British commissioner did not follow the lead of his American colleague in this regard. While he was content to rely on the reasons he had advanced in that earlier judgment in so far as they related to the clash of legal approaches to the institution of slavery in cases of distress,[109] he decided that he should take the opportunity to address the "peculiar circumstances"[110] in which the *Creole* had entered Nassau Harbor in November of 1841. These, he believed, materially distinguished the two cases.

To Commissioner Hornby, the "gravamen"—the very essence—of the American claim in the *Creole* case was that the slaves on board had secured their liberty through the interference of the British colonial authorities in the Bahamas.[111] This, he asserted, flew in the face of the facts, which demonstrated that the mutineers "had, on their arrival at Nassau, the sole and exclusive possession and custody of the crew as well as of the vessel, the former being their prisoners."[112] Consequently, "the relation of master and slave never in fact existed within British jurisdiction, it having been forcibly dissolved on board the 'Creole' by the slaves themselves."[113] Though Madison Washington and his fellow mutineers had used violence to secure their freedom, there had been no violation of international law or the law applicable in the colony.[114] It followed, in Hornby's view, that "there exists no obligation on the part of Great Britain to surrender them."[115]

Unlike the facts in the *Enterprize* case, in this instance, there had been no "continuance of the custody of the slaves,"[116] from the high seas to the British colonial harbor. Nor, in the view of the British commissioner, had this situation changed in the days which followed its arrival. It is true, as detailed in chapter 1 of this study, that troops from the West India Regiment had swiftly been sent aboard by Governor Cockburn to maintain order and to provide the conditions for an investigation into the alleged offenses to be undertaken by the local authorities—both actions having the explicit assent of the US consul. Did these actions serve to alter the preexisting legal position of the mutineers or other (formerly) enslaved persons on board? In the words of Hornby: "In the course of the argument it was stated that, when the guard came on board, the mutiny had ceased, and then we are asked to infer that the crew had recovered possession of the brig and control over the slaves; but it is impossible for us to do this, in as much as the evidence distinctly shows that the crew never did, in fact, get the upper hand."[117] Indeed, the "authorities at Nassau could have no right to interpose by force to reduce the individuals . . . again into a state of slavery not tolerated by the laws of Great Britain."[118] The commissioner might well have explored this in greater depth as under the Slave Trade Act of 1824,[119] as amended;[120] to so act would arguably have constituted a serious criminal offense carrying with it the most severe of penalties.[121] It was the conclusion of the commissioner that during this immediate post-arrival period, the mutineers remained in possession of the *Creole* and in control of its passengers and crew.

In the same context, the commissioner turned his attention to the converse of the above; namely, that the authorities in Nassau equally "could not permit the interposition of any other persons" with the interest to reduce the mutineers and their colleagues to a state of slavery while the *Creole* was within a British port.[122] This issue had arisen for consideration as a consequence of the submissions of John A. Thomas, the agent and counsel for the United States, before the tribunal.

It concerns "the strange development of the plot concerted by American citizens, under the direction of the American consul, in a time of profound national peace, to take the Creole and her negroes by force, from the jurisdiction of the British laws, under the protection and control of which they were lying."[123] In essence, the plan, as seen above, was to take control by force and to spirit the brig to Indian Key in Florida where there was believed to be a US naval vessel which could afford it protection.

Mention of this most curious plot was, as noted in chapter 1 and in the discussion of the Louisiana insurance cases above, largely absent from the diplomatic and other records generated in Nassau at the time. Nor, indeed, did it form part of the statement of facts, set out at some length, in the formal protest submitted by the American envoy in London to the British Foreign Secretary on 1 March 1842.[124] Rather, one must turn to the controversial joint formal sworn protest lodged by various of the crew and passengers upon the arrival of the *Creole* in New Orleans in December of 1841 for details.[125]

That source reveals that at the time of its arrival in Nassau two other American merchant vessels, the *Louisa* and the *Congress,* were also at anchor in the harbor. Within hours, it had been agreed between the officers of the *Creole,* the American consul, and the captain of the *Louisa* that an attempt should be made to take control and set sail for the United States.[126] This plan was further refined by the parties, including the consul, in the course of the next two days. Finally, on Friday, November 12, it was set in motion.[127] Captain Woodside, with an armed American crew drawn from the other two vessels, rowed towards their target. In the words of the New Orleans Protest:

> The muskets and cutlasses were obtained from the brig Congress. Every effort had been made, in concert with the American consul, to purchase arms of [*sic*] the dealers at Nassau, but they all refused to sell. The arms were wrapped in the American flag, and concealed in the bottom of the boat. As said boat approached the Creole, a negro in a boat who had watched the loading of the boat, followed her and gave the alarm to the British officer in command on board the Creole; and as the boat came up to the Creole, the officer called to them, "Keep off, or I will fire into you." His company of twenty-four men were then all standing on deck, and drawn up in line fronting Captain Woodside's boat, and were ready, with loaded muskets and fixed bayonets, for an engagement. Captain Woodside was thus forced to withdraw from the Creole, and the plan was prevented from being executed.[128]

The deponents, in concluding upon this matter, stated that it was this interference "which prevented aid from being rendered by the American sailors in Nassau, and caused the loss of the slaves to their owners."[129]

Commissioner Hornby was at a loss to understand the logic of the American agent in raising this matter in his submissions. He opined, "The British authorities were bound to interfere to prevent its accom-

plishment, and if this is the 'interference' which worked the emancipation complained of, and there is no other pretence of interference, the
simple statement of the facts will be sufficient to demonstrate its absur-
dity."[130] The plot was, in his view, "palpably at variance with the law
of nations."[131] It is to be regretted that Hornby did not also take the
opportunity to explore whether the admitted conspiracy and the acts in
furtherance of that conspiracy, could be regarded as proof of wanton and
serious acts of criminality on the part of those concerned.[132]

There is one further dimension to the judgment of the British commissioner which is of relevance for present purposes: his views on the
international law doctrine concerning the status of vessels entering foreign
ports in distress. Building upon his opinion rendered in the case of the
Enterprize, Hornby stressed his acceptance of the right of the vessels of
all nations, to enter foreign ports and harbors in distress "and to retain,
to some extent at least, and for some purposes . . . the laws of the country
from which the vessel derives a national character."[133] This principle,
properly understood, was—as he had stressed in that earlier instance—
subject to exceptions, and was not applicable in the circumstances of
the present case. The rule was, he opined, derived from "the ordinary
necessities of commerce, and can have nothing to do with the relations
existing between man and man, except where such relations are the result
of contracts entered into by means of their own free will."[134] Furthermore,
the immunity from the exercise of port state jurisdiction did not apply in
the face of post-entry criminal conduct. In his opinion, "slavery being, as
against the individual held in bondage, a continuous wrong every moment that he was so held, was an offence against the laws of the country
in which the individual holding him was thus accidentally territorially
situated, and therefore punishable by and under those laws."[135]

The reasoning advanced by Hornby in his judgment did not find a
receptive audience in Umpire Joshua Bates. In his award, rendered on
9 January 1855, but a week before the expiration of his mandate, he held
comprehensively in favor of the United States. It is reproduced in full,
for ease of reference, in appendix 3. It would be fair to say that in both
his articulation of the facts and in the formulation of his conclusions as

to the nature of the international law rule he embraced the most extreme positions which emerged from the American narrative.

In relation to his view of the facts, he was clearly influenced by those set out by the crew and passengers of the *Creole* in the December 1841 protest in New Orleans though this source was not explicitly referenced by him.[136] Nor does the award acknowledge the controversy which surrounded its contents and the earlier judicial criticism of the same in both the Vice-Admiralty Court of the Bahamas in 1842 and the Supreme Court of Louisiana in 1845.

In the recitation of the facts, as he saw them, Bates emphasized that when, on 9 November 1841, following his first meeting with Governor Cockburn, the US consul "went on board the brig, placed the mate in command in place of the disabled master, and found the slaves all quiet." During the "whole time" thereafter that the troops, magistrates and other local authorities were on board "they encouraged the insubordination of the slaves." On Friday 12 November a large number of persons in boats arrived with "bludgeons" and clubs assembled in the near of the *Creole:* "They were under the immediate command of the pilot who took the vessel into the port—who was an officer of the Government—and a co-loured man." Furthermore, "a vast concourse of people were collected on shore opposite the brig."

In this intimidating context, the Attorney General of the Bahamas came aboard. Having ordered the removal of the 19 ringleaders, he had liberated the remaining slaves. Assisted by the Bahamian magistrates, they were taken on board the adjacent small boats "and when landed, were conducted by a vast assemblage to the Superintendent of Police, by whom their names were registered." In the view of the umpire, "[t]hey were thus forcibly taken from the custody of the master of the 'Creole' and lost to the claimants." Of the contrary British narrative of all of these events, summarized in chapter 1, there is no mention.

The voyage of the *Creole* was, Bates opined, one sanctioned by the laws of the United States and was not contrary to the law of nations. It followed that she had "the right to seek shelter or enter the ports of a friendly power in case of distress or any unavoidable necessity." In the circumstances, the British colonial authorities were duty-bound to take the necessary steps to facilitate the return of the mutineers and the remaining slaves to the United States.

Given what has been said above, it is no surprise that the overall conclusion of the umpire was a sweeping one and that his finding was fully in favor of the American claim. In his words:

> The municipal law of England cannot authorize a magistrate to violate the law of nations, by invading with an armed force the vessel of a friendly nation that has committed no offence, and forcibly dissolving the relations which, by the laws of his country, the captain is bound to preserve and enforce on board. These rights, sanctioned by the law of nations, viz, the right to navigate the ocean and to seek shelter in case of distress or other unavoidable circumstances, and to retain over the ship, her cargo, and passengers, the laws of her own country, must be respected by all nations, for no independent nation would submit to their violation.

It followed that "the claimants are justly entitled to compensation for their losses." The near fourteen-year quest of Thomas McCargo, and the other affected slavers, for full financial redress was thus brought to a successful conclusion.

The award by Bates of \$110,330[137] in the *Creole* case was the largest made by the mixed-claims tribunal and amounted to nearly one-third of the total made on behalf of all United States claimants.[138] The awards were promptly satisfied.[139] Many of the more important and complex disputes were, in the final event, referred to Bates for decision. As has been pointed out elsewhere, this "rendered his labors arduous, and his responsibility great. Although provision was made in the treaty to compensate him for his services, yet he refused to receive any remuneration whatever."[140]

The *Creole* Award: A Persuasive Precedent?

In contrast to the judgment of the Supreme Court of Louisiana in the *Mc-Cargo* insurance case, which has continued to attract periodic attention due to the compelling human factors which arose for consideration in it, the award of Umpire Bates in settling (for the purposes of the dispute in question), without right of appeal, the international law position in relation to the distress rule has had a more profound and lasting impact. Indeed, it has continued to be cited with approval—though often without detailed analysis and with diminishing frequency—by international law scholars up to the present day. The question which arises is whether it is truly worthy of this positive treatment.

Several factors point to the need to subject this award to critical scrutiny though the first of these extends well beyond the somewhat idiosyncratic manner in which the umpire saw fit to marshal the facts and to express his conclusions. As noted at an earlier stage of this chapter, Article I of the treaty of 1853 authorized the commissioners and the umpire to determine the issues before them on the basis of "justice and equity" (*ex aequo et bono*) rather than on grounds of international law alone. The granting of this latitude to the decision-makers at this point in the evolution of international adjudication was by no means unusual. Merrills and De Brabandere have remarked, "These early Anglo-American commissions were not judicial tribunals in the modern sense, but were supposed to blend juridical with diplomatic considerations to produce (in effect) a negotiated settlement."[141] As Neff reminds us, "[t]he connection between arbitration and international law is not so close as might be initially supposed."[142] Bates, it will be recalled, was a banker and not a jurist. The selection of non-lawyers as arbitrators was not unusual at that time;[143] a practice made more understandable given the nature of the mandate which had been afforded.

A second factor of significance relates to disputes of a maritime nature. Throughout the 19th Century the law of the sea was in a constant state of evolution and found substance in the unwritten rules of customary international law. These were, by their nature, often difficult to divine from the developing state practice which gave them birth. Greater certainty had to await the codification of this branch of the Law of Nations in the second half of the 20th Century. In the 1840s, however, there was a broad consensus that the greater part of the oceans—the high seas—were free and open to all states for the purposes of navigation and fishing. Similarly, it was agreed—and beyond dispute—that the state of registry of a vessel whilst on the high seas (the flag state) enjoyed exclusive jurisdiction thereon. Similarly, it was broadly accepted that coastal states were entitled to a belt of maritime territory, known as the territorial sea, projecting seaward from the shore in which they could exercise a range of rights subject to the need to respect the innocent passage of foreign vessels. However, for many years there remained doubts both as to maximum permitted width of this maritime zone and as to its precise juridical nature.[144] It was also largely accepted that the waters landward of the baselines from which the territorial sea is measured, such as estuaries and ports, were subject to a more complete submission to the interests of the coastal state. As Lee reminds us, these waters "are assimilated to the land territory and are not subject to the right of innocent passage by foreign vessels."[145] It is this latter aspect of the law of the sea—one which remains uncodified to the present day—which is primarily engaged by the fact circumstances of the *Creole* incident.

It is beyond doubt that, as a consequence of such assimilation, the coastal state has a general right to close its ports to foreign vessels, to nominate those which are to be open to international trade, and to prescribe conditions for access.[146] When, as with Nassau Harbor in November 1841, a foreign merchant vessel voluntarily enters, the question of the exercise of jurisdiction over activities on board necessarily arises.

Two schools of thought came to pervade the practice of states on this matter. The first, most commonly associated with France, adopted the position that "the coastal State has in law no jurisdiction over purely internal affairs of foreign ships in its ports."[147] The second, the Anglo-American approach, stresses that by entering foreign ports, vessels place themselves within the jurisdiction of the coastal state though it may elect to refrain from its exercise in certain circumstances relating to the internal economy of the vessel.[148]

The British position was summarized in 1929 in a formal submission to the Preparatory Committee of The Hague Codification Conference. As a general rule, it asserted that "the State is entitled to exercise jurisdiction over a foreign merchant vessel lying in its ports and over persons and goods on board."[149] However, it acknowledged that it was common to forego the exercise of such authority in favor of the concurrent jurisdiction of the flag state. For instance, the submission noted that in criminal matters it was "not unusual" for the local authorities to decline to intervene, in the absence of a request so to do, "unless the peace or good order of the port is likely to be affected. In every case, it is for the authorities of the State to judge whether or not to intervene."[150]

The American position was to like effect. In the words of the US Supreme Court in *Cunard v. Mellon:*

> A merchant ship of one country voluntarily entering the territorial limits of another subjects herself to the jurisdiction of the latter. The jurisdiction attaches in virtue of her presence, just as with other objects within those limits. During her stay she is entitled to the protection of the laws of that place and correlatively is bound to yield obedience to them. Of course, the local sovereign may out of considerations of public policy choose to forego the exertion of its jurisdiction or to exert the same in only a limited way, but this is a matter resting solely in its discretion.[151]

American doctrine on the exercise of jurisdiction with respect to crime also broadly mirrored that of the United Kingdom.[152] The emphasis afforded to the jurisdictional autonomy of the flag state while in a foreign port by Secretary of State Webster in his letter to Lord Ashburton of 1 August 1842 relating to the *Creole*[153] is thus somewhat at variance with the preponderant approach of his country viewed over time and has, as a consequence, attracted scholarly criticism.[154] Modern customary law, it might be noted, favors the Anglo-American doctrine.[155]

While under the general rules explored above, coastal states enjoy the right to regulate access to their ports and harbors, the stark realities of the perils of the seas gave rise to the need for an exception to their application. McDougal and Burke have remarked: "The one customary right of access, quite universally accepted arises from the humanitarian obligation to admit vessels in distress because of the weather or damage to the vessel."[156] This view is broadly shared and is evident in the practice of states and the decisions of domestic courts and international tribunals.[157] In the words of the *North Atlantic Coast Fisheries* case, decided in 1910 by the Permanent Court of Arbitration in The Hague, it is one of "those duties of hospitality and humanity which all civilized nations impose upon themselves and expect the performance of from others."[158] This "safe harbor" rule is not, it should be stressed, confined to instances of adverse weather. As was stated in the *Kate A. Hoff* arbitration of 1929, it is "generally stated to apply to vessels forced into port by storm, or compelled to seek refuge for vital repairs or provisioning, or carried into port by mutineers."[159] The *force majeure* and distress exceptions,[160] so conceived, were thus sufficiently broad in scope to embrace the fact circumstances of the *Creole* incident.

A critical and associated issue then necessarily arises; namely, the extent to which a vessel seeking shelter in such circumstances attracts immunity from the operation of the laws and regulations of the coastal state.[161] Some commentators have asserted that the protection derived from the operation of the rule is encyclopedic. Jessup, notably, utilizes such an absolute formulation. He opined that "an entire immunity" resulted. He continued, "If a ship is driven in by storm, carried in by mutineers, or seeks refuge for vital repairs or provisioning, international customary law declares that the local state shall not take advantage of its necessity."[162] The awards of Umpire Bates in the cases of the *Hermosa,* the *Enterprize,* and the *Creole* are consistent with this expansive approach to immunity. In the proceedings relating to the *Enterprize,* for example, the submissions of the American agent contained no acknowledgement of any exceptions to the distress rule which was formulated in absolute terms.[163] The judgment of the US commissioner and the award of the umpire similarly failed to engage with notions of limitations on the scope of its operation. The award in the *Creole* case did not depart from this stance.

This view of the scope of the safe harbor exception, however, sits uneasily with some other authorities. One such example is to be found in the *María Luz* arbitral award of 1875, which is reproduced, for convenience, in appendix 4. Le Moli reminds us, "On 9 July 1872, the *María Luz*, a Peruvian cargo ship carrying 230 bonded Chinese labourers from Macao, docked in the Japanese port of Yokohama, after being damaged in a storm. The ship needed to refit before proceeding to its destination in Peru. A few days later, while the ship was anchored in the port, one of the Chinese labourers leaped overboard and sought refuge on a British ship, HMS *Iron Duke*."[164] This set in train a series of events, including an investigation of the deplorable conditions, akin to slavery, in which the laborers were held and the institution by the Japanese authorities of civil and criminal proceedings. As Crawford has stated, "[a]s a result of the judicial ruling, the Chinese coolies went free, and Captain Hereira departed from Japan, abandoning both the *María Luz* and her crew."[165]

These facts formed the basis for a Peruvian claim that Japan had violated international law and should pay compensation. In the summer of 1873, following bilateral negotiations, it was agreed to submit the dispute to the czar of Russia for a final and conclusive arbitral determination.[166] Such "sovereign" arbitration was by no means unknown.[167] However, as a dispute settlement mechanism, it had several drawbacks. One such was that the head of state would rarely provide detailed reasons for the award.[168] Furthermore, it was common for the arbitrator to seek advice or, in effect, to delegate the decision-making task to a subordinate.[169] Both of these features were present in this 1875 case.[170]

It is clear from the detailed research on this case recently subject to analysis by Colombo that questions of public international law, including the distress rule, were extensively treated in the submissions of the parties.[171] Indeed, the award of the umpire in the *Creole* case was explicitly brought to the attention of the arbitrator.[172] Nonetheless, in his award of May 1875, Alexander II, emperor of all the Russias, concluded in favor of

Japan. In his view, "the Japanese government acted in good faith (*bona fide*) in virtue of its own laws and customs, without infringing the general prescriptions of the law of nations, or the stipulations of particular treaties."

Given its brevity, it was perhaps inevitable that there would be disagreement as to the awards' meaning and importance. At one end of the spectrum, Charteris asserts that it stands as authority "that a state in which slavery was expressly forbidden was entitled to enforce its prohibitions and set free slaves carried on a foreign vessel within the limits of its territory."[173] From Jessup—in stark contrast and rather unconvincingly—comes the conclusion that "[i]n view of the special circumstances of this case it cannot be considered opposed to the general doctrine of immunity derived from forced entrance."[174]

It should be noted in this context that considerable authority exists to the effect that the immunity flowing from the application of the distress rule is not absolute but subject to limitations and exceptions. By way of illustration, to Oppenheim vessels entering ports in distress enjoy "a certain immunity from the local jurisdiction."[175] To the international law scholars who in 1929 compiled, under the auspices of the Harvard Law School, a draft convention on territorial waters, vessels in distress "may not wholly ignore the local jurisdiction."[176] Certain judicial decisions point in the same direction. For instance in the *Kate A. Hoff* arbitration of 1929 the arbitrators speak of the distress rule exempting a merchant vessel "at least to a certain extent, from the operation of local laws."[177] In *Cushan and Lewis* v. *The King*, the Canadian courts cautioned that the distress principle "must not be too widely interpreted."[178]

Perhaps the example most frequently offered as an exception to the distress rule concerns the application of the criminal law of the coastal state.[179] In the words of the commentary to the Harvard draft convention, "if the vessel or those on board commit an offense against the local law subsequent to the entry in distress, the littoral state's power to punish is undiminished."[180] An alternative way of considering the criminal law question is to recall that one of the purposes of the distress rule is to ensure that the coastal state cannot take advantage of the involuntary entry in question. This would, *per force*, insulate pre-entry conduct from the operation of the laws of the coastal state. However, criminal conduct subsequent to entry falls logically outside the scope of the rationale for safe harbor protection and should thus be treated under the general rules concerning the operation of the criminal laws of the port state discussed above.[181]

As was noted earlier in this chapter, the British Commissioner, Hornby, embraced the criminal law exception view in his judgments in both the *Enterprize* and *Creole* cases though neither award by the umpire engaged with this matter. It is of some importance to recall, however, that in the diplomatic record of the *Creole* mutiny, there are to be found distinct echoes of the criminal law exception in the stance adopted by the United States.

By way of illustration, in the official American protest to the United Kingdom government of 1 March 1842, the validity of the criminal law exception was explicitly conceded. In the words of Edward Everett: "If any act violating British law had been committed on board the '*Creole*' while in the port of Nassau, the authorities might lawfully interfere to repress or punish it. If any aid were asked of these authorities by the officers of the '*Creole*' for an unlawful purpose, that aid would of course be withheld."[182] A similar but more abbreviated conclusion is contained in the letter from Secretary of State Webster to Lord Ashburton dated 1 August 1842.[183] It is of relevance to recall that in the previous month, Webster had seen fit to involve the attorney general of the United States, Hugh S. Legaré, in his discussions with Ashburton concerning the *Creole* issue. On July 20, at the request of the latter, the attorney committed his views as to the legal position to writing.[184] He opined, in part, as follows: "The principle is, that if a vessel be driven by stress of weather, or forced by *vis major*, or, in short, be compelled by any overruling necessity to take refuge in the ports of another, she is not considered as subject to the municipal law of that other, so far as concerns any penalty, prohibition, tax, or incapacity that would otherwise be incurred by entering the ports; provided she do nothing further to violate the municipal law during her stay."[185]

As noted earlier, Commissioner Hornby had concluded that the holding of persons in bondage in the Bahamas without lawful authority was a criminal offense and had a continuing quality. Similarly, he had asserted that, as a consequence of that law, the local authorities were precluded from using force to reduce those on board once again to a state of slavery. Both of these scenarios were arguably within the rule as expounded by Everett. The American envoy, by contrast, found in the circumstances of the *Creole* incident "absolutely nothing to furnish a lawful ground of interference . . . in order to effect the liberation of the slaves."[186] It is to be regretted that this important divergence of views relevant to the proper characterization of this aspect of the dispute was ignored by the umpire in his award.[187]

It should be stressed that in none of the above American formulations of the criminal law exception to the distress rule, were the actions of the US consul, jointly with others, to take control of the *Creole* by force alluded to. As we have seen, this plot was foiled by the British troops which had been sent on board, with the consent of the consul, to maintain order and to facilitate an investigation of the mutiny by British officials. It goes without saying that whilst aboard the *Creole* for these purposes the actions of the troops and local officials were governed by the laws in force in the colony of the Bahamas. Similarly, as consent negatives the possibility of legal wrong, their presence for these purposes could not constitute a violation of the Law of Nations.[188]

As we have seen, the plot by the consul in concert with other American citizens to seize control of the *Creole* was raised for consideration by the US agent to the arbitration proceedings and was invoked by Umpire Bates in his award. Curiously, this was not done in what might be thought to be the orthodox manner: namely, as evidence of a possible criminal conspiracy and acts in furtherance of that conspiracy. While the award lacks clarity and precision in this context, Bates appears to have regarded the acts in question as an appropriate initiative to prevent the slaves from being taken from the "custody" of the officers of the *Creole* and being lost to their owners. As to the status of the troops sent aboard, the umpire fails to acknowledge or address the notion or relevance of "consent." Rather, he characterized their presence and actions as an aspect of the invasion of the vessel "with an armed force," a conclusion which some may well feel is far from self-evidently sound.[189]

Various commentators have raised further criticisms of the *Creole* award or of the view of the distress rule which it embodies. Some, such as Piggott (having considered in particular the July 1842 opinion of the US Attorney General), have argued that the American formulation of the distress rule was overly wide.[190] Others, including O'Connell, have drawn attention to the fact that the safe harbor rule had, in its origins, a strictly humanitarian purpose whereas, in the *Creole*, it had been afforded a clearly contrary application.[191]

Furthermore, Corbett is not alone in suggesting that the distress rule was, at the relevant time, merely one of comity which had yet to crystalize into an obligatory norm of customary international law. Having specifically referenced, *inter alia,* the *Creole* incident, he wrote thus: "Notwithstanding that this principle is frequently cited with approval, it would seem that such an immunity is not well founded, or in any sense obligatory; and that whilst putting into port under constraint might be a good ground in comity for excusing such infringements of local regulations as were due to the exigencies of her position, it would certainly not carry any legal right to exemption from the local law or local jurisdiction."[192] The distinction in question is an important one. As Kämmerer reminds us, "[t]he notion of international comity encompasses forms of conduct in relations between sovereign States which are based on courtesy, tradition, goodwill, or utility. Though not being legally binding, comity is enshrined as rules, albeit of tradition or usage, and not of international law."[193] It may be of interest to recall that in some of the most significant communications in the early phases of this dispute, both between governments and internally, the American authorities had a tendency to use these terms seemingly interchangeably.[194]

In light of all that has been said above, it would seem to be both unsafe and unsatisfactory to regard the award rendered by Umpire Bates in the case of the *Creole* in January 1855 as a persuasive articulation of the relevant rules of the customary international law of the sea either in the mid-19th century or now.

Chapter 5

Concluding Reflections

When, in early December 1841, the *Creole* finally arrived in the "Crescent City," minus most of its human "cargo," and its crew and passengers formulated the New Orleans Protest, it engendered a febrile atmosphere in the media, in southern political circles, and among sections of the population at large.[1] As has been noted elsewhere: "The *Creole* mutiny electrified the nation and helped escalate sectional tensions over slavery. Southerners (and some northerners) were outraged that British authorities chose to free US slaves, especially those who had taken violent action against their masters. They viewed the British as endorsing slave insurrections—their worst nightmare—while also denying Americans their legal right to the domestic slave trade."[2] Some called for the United States to resort to armed force in reprisal.[3] Certain commentators have even argued that the mutiny and its aftermath brought Britain and America to the brink of war.[4] This characterization seems unwarranted. Although the American envoy in London, in his official protest to Lord Aberdeen of 1 March 1842, expressly pressed upon the British authorities "a full conviction of the most dangerous importance to the peace of the two countries of occurrences of this description, and the questions to which they give rise"[5] it was evident that the Tyler administration did not regard the *Creole* incident, standing alone, as a *casus belli*.

At the other end of the spectrum of scholarly commentary, some have appeared to minimize the importance of this affair. To Levy, for instance, the *Creole* incident caused but "a minor diplomatic storm."[6] The truth, this study suggests, is somewhat more nuanced. As noted in chapter 3, the events off the island of Abaco and thereafter in Nassau Harbor in November 1841 took place at a time of heightened tensions between these two English-speaking superpowers and on the eve of the launch of a major diplomatic initiative designed to reset that important relationship. The mutiny by Madison Washington and his colleagues made that task yet more difficult. Viewed in that broader context, the *Creole* incident "held great potential for trouble."[7]

That the *Creole* affair was so considered is made manifest by the extent to which some of the most senior political and diplomatic figures of the day devoted their time and energy to quelling the anxieties to which it had given rise and in seeking to limit the possibility of a similar recurrence. This is no better illustrated than in the interactions between Lord Ashburton and Secretary of State Webster in their many months of negotiations in Washington, DC, in 1842. The record reveals that the discussions over the *Creole* affair were detailed, time-consuming, and difficult, notwithstanding the fact that the issue of financial compensation was left to one side. The end result was, as this study has demonstrated, more favorable to the British position in so far as *Creole*-related matters were concerned than to that of the United States. It was also evident that both countries were reluctant to let it compromise their efforts to secure the greatest prize then in issue between them: namely, the settlement of the northeastern boundary between the United States and the possessions of the Crown in what is now Canada. In this, it was successful, the treaty being widely regarded as a milestone in the creation of the stable, enduring, and largely undefended frontier separating these North American neighbors.

As we have seen, the starting point of Secretary of State Webster concerning the *Creole* was that the treaty then in contemplation should include specific provisions inspired by the mutiny: namely, on the issue of the extradition of fugitive offenders and on affording greater security of navigation for American merchant vessels in Bahamian waters. It is true that, in the end, the Webster–Ashburton Treaty re-established arrangements between the two countries for extradition: a basic form of international cooperation in criminal matters which had previously existed between them but had fallen into abeyance. However, the agreement reached was narrow in scope, and the limited list of extraditable offenses did not include those most relevant to the fact circumstances of that revolt as conceived by Webster. Indeed, the United States would have to wait until 1889 before it could secure "'revolt' onboard a ship on the high seas" as an extradition offense in its relations with Great Britain and its wider Empire.[8] President Tyler, in his submission of the treaty for consideration by the Senate, stressed the importance of the extradition provisions in relations with Canada.[9] Of the *Creole,* there was no direct mention.

The negotiations on American demands for greater security for its vessels against British "interference" yielded even more disappointing results for Washington. In this regard, the treaty was silent. The undertakings by Lord Ashburton as to the future were, as revealed in chapter 3, both modest and embodied in an exchange of notes rather than in the treaty itself.[10] As we have seen, even the limited central undertaking given by the British special envoy was neither embraced with enthusiasm by London nor implemented with promptitude.

Security of navigation in the Bahama Channel was by no means the only irritant in relations to be discussed by Webster and Ashburton, where the results were destined to be embodied in an exchange of notes between them. As mentioned previously, the burning and destruction of the American vessel *Caroline* at Niagara by a British raiding party in 1837, with associated loss of life, had given rise to tensions which had simmered over the ensuing years.[11] The matter had escalated more recently with the arrest in New York State and subsequent prosecution of one Mr. McLeod for murder, for his alleged role in that incident.[12] Diplomatic exchanges were revived in the spring of 1841, but the matter remained open and therefore had to be taken forward by Ashburton. Those discussions resulted in an agreement between the two states on the American formulation of the principles underlying the proper exercise of the right of self-defense in international law, though they continued to differ in their applicability to the facts of the incident in question.[13] This formulation of the rule of self-defense remains among the best known to international legal scholarship[14] and continues to be invoked with frequency, especially in relation to anticipatory action and defense against non-state actors.[15] Interestingly, the claim of Mr. McLeod for compensation for his treatment was subsequently submitted to the mixed-claims commission. On 5 January 1855—four days prior to the *Creole* award—Umpire Bates rejected it on the grounds that the matter had been amicably settled by diplomatic means in 1841 and 1842.[16]

Webster appears to have been broadly content with the overall outcome of his negotiations with Ashburton. In so far as the *Creole* was concerned, while the results fell short of what he had wished for, the adopted approach had permitted public and political passions to cool and for tensions to abate. More positively, the case for compensation remained open, to be taken forward in the regular course of bilateral diplomacy. Shortly before he demitted office as Secretary of State in 1843, he wrote to Everett, still the American envoy in London: "Nothing gives me more satisfaction in leaving this Department, than the humble trust that the questions which have existed between the two countries, and which have been subjects of discussion since I came into office, will be found to have been settled in a manner honourable to both, likely to promote harmony and good will between them, and to preserve the peace of the world."[17] In the years which followed, Webster continued his distinguished career of public service, first as a US senator for Massachusetts and then, yet again, as secretary of state, during which period he passed away in office. As Howe reminds us, "[w]hen Webster died, President Millard Fillmore . . . appointed Everett secretary of state for the last four months" of his term.[18]

Ashburton returned to a life of retirement in England. His efforts to restore Anglo-American relations were appreciated on both sides of the Atlantic. Everett informed the Foreign Secretary on 15 September 1842:

"All my letters from home concur in the warmest commendations of the manner in which Lord Ashburton has discharged his highly responsible trust."[19] At home, the British government regarded his efforts on its behalf in a positive light. However, that relationship soon soured in a quintessentially English—though thankfully private—exchange of correspondence on the award of honors and distinctions to mark his service to the Crown.[20] Alexander Baring, a mere baron, was offered preferment in the order of precedence to the rank of viscount rather than to the more elevated status of earl. This he declined. On 26 October 1842, Aberdeen (himself an earl) wrote, by way of explanation, in part, as follows: "When I recollect our situation with respect to the United States this time last year, and compare it with our present position, in my opinion a Dukedom would not be disproportioned to the service performed. But this is an affair which must be regulated in some degree by precedent, and by the peculiar circumstances of the case."[21] The style and title offered, he added, had been regarded as appropriate by the Duke of Wellington—"a great master of Honours"—and by the Queen.[22] Baron Ashburton was unmoved.[23] Aberdeen continued to prosper thereafter remaining as foreign secretary until 1846. Unlike Webster, who never realized his presidential ambitions, he eventually rose to the apex of the British political system, serving as prime minister from 1852 to 1855.

As noted, the Webster–Ashburton negotiations put to one side the issue of financial compensation. In this regard, the slavers first turned to the courts of Louisiana in their efforts to force the insurance industry to indemnify them against loss. In the ensuing litigation, much turned on a judicial assessment of the underlying fact circumstances of the mutiny and its immediate aftermath. Posterity (though not the majority of the slave owners) was fortunate that the matter came to be determined by Justice Henry Bullard. A highly intelligent and experienced judge, his pivotal decision in *McCargo* v. *New Orleans Insurance Co.*[24] was, in its marshaling of the facts, a near model of clarity, balance, and professionalism. The underlying issues of insurance law which he addressed in this and related appeals were somewhat less challenging and his conclusions on points of law have, as a consequence, been but infrequently invoked.

As to the man himself, he demitted judicial office not long afterwards and in 1847 was appointed professor of civil law at the University of Louisiana.[25] Upon his death in 1851, his accomplishments were memorialized by the membership of the Bar at New Orleans. Those present unanimously resolved, *inter alia,* "[t]hat as a jurist he was learned and profound without pedantry, and as a scholar accomplished and refined without ostentation."[26] His continued standing in legal circles is perhaps well illustrated by the fact that his portrait, painted by Thomas C. Healy in 1843 (see fig. 9), today still adorns the Trial Moot Court Room at Tulane Law School.

The Louisiana insurance litigation also helped to consolidate the growing reputations of two of the attorneys who were most heavily involved. One was Thomas Slidell, a Yale graduate, who went on to become an associate justice of the supreme court of the state and eventually its chief justice. The other was the relatively youthful Judah P. Benjamin. Aided in no small measure by his involvement—on behalf of various insurance companies—in the *Creole* cases, his professional rise was to prove to be meteoric.[27] As Chief Justice Bermudez of Louisiana was to recall upon Benjamin's death in 1884, "[t]o his clients he was infallible."[28] As is well-known, Benjamin went on to establish an extensive practice before the Supreme Court of the United States while simultaneously serving as a US senator for Louisiana. In the Civil War, he sided with the Confederacy and was a constant and influential presence in the cabinet of Jefferson Davis. In political exile in London thereafter, he enjoyed a glittering—if relatively brief—career at the English Bar.[29]

The judgment of Justice Bullard in *McCargo* v. *New Orleans Insurance Co.* was, as noted earlier, well-crafted and persuasively argued. It was based on a detailed, logical, and balanced examination of the facts to which his understanding of the relevant law and associated authorities was applied in a clear and coherent manner. It stands in stark contrast to the international arbitral award handed down by Umpire Bates on 9 January 1855.[30] As was seen in chapter 4, his articulation of the facts of the *Creole* mutiny was partial and unbalanced, failing as it did to engage in any meaningful fashion with the alternative British narrative with which he had been presented. His treatment of international legal issues was extremely brief. Having claimed to have "read all of the authorities" referred to by both parties, his award contained only one substantive reference to either scholarly commentary or case law authority; namely, a citation to the relatively controversial doctrine of the direct incorporation of customary international law into the *corpus* of the common law of England.[31] His application of the law to the facts was, at best, haphazard. It could be said on his behalf, however, that he was working under extreme pressure of time as his mandate was due to expire within days. In his biographical sketch of Bates, Orbell notes that as early as 3 February 1855, he expressed regret "that 'more time was not given me to perfect my decisions' which, he reckoned, 'would cut a poor figure alongside the more elaborate opinions of the learned commissioners.'"[32] He was right to be concerned. As this study has previously concluded, it would be unsafe and unsatisfactory to regard his judgment as a persuasive articulation of the then relevant international law rules.

It may come as some relief to know that, as a consequence of the progressive intrusion of considerations of human rights and fundamental freedoms into the fabric of the international legal system throughout the 20th century, such an outcome could not plausibly be replicated in the most unlikely event that the same facts as those of the *Creole* were ever to manifest themselves again. It is beyond doubt that customary international law has evolved so as to contain a prohibition of slavery.[33] Indeed, it can be argued with some conviction that this new rule has attained the status of a fundamental norm of that legal system. By way of illustration, the influential International Law Commission of the United Nations in 2022 characterized the prohibition of slavery (and not merely the slave trade) as but one of only eight rules of the international legal order possessing the status of peremptory norms (*jus cogens*) which are "universally applicable" and "hierarchically superior" to all others.[34] One cannot but agree with Churchill and Lowe who have remarked that "it is most unlikely that the monstrous illegality of slavery would today be considered to be protected by the essentially humanitarian distress rule."[35] It should also be stressed that the judgment by Bates was not slavery-specific. In the *Creole* award, as with those relating to the *Enterprize* and the *Hermosa,* the underlying customary law rule in question was permitting the involuntary entry of vessels in distress to the ports of foreign states. The vagaries of the weather and the perils of the seas continue to ensure that merchantmen will, on occasion, seek safe harbor. This study suggests that the absolutist view of the relevant associated norms relating to jurisdiction adopted by Bates in this context should also be treated with both considerable caution and appropriate skepticism.

The Umpire claimed his decision was based on "the established law of nations." As previously noted, however, the scope of his actual authority was much broader, in effect permitting him to make his determinations on the basis of "justice and equity"[36] or *ex aequo et bono.* Had Bates invoked this broader remit, his award would perhaps have been slightly more convincing in terms of its outcome. From the outset, the American authorities had argued it would, in the overall context of the relations between the two countries, be unjust for the *Creole* slavers to be left without compensation while the British emancipation legislation, which entered into force in 1834, had ensured that slave owners in the Bahamas would receive full recompense for the loss of their human "property."[37] Similarly, in the case of the *Enterprize* Upham, the US Commissioner, remarked that "the act abolishing slavery acknowledged the legality and validity of slavery as an institution, as it rendered compensation for the liberation of slaves according to their respective valuations, and also gave to the owners of slaves the benefit of a term of intermediate service. If it was not considered right to liberate *British* slaves except on these conditions, how can it be right to compel the liberation of *American* slaves, casually thrown within the country, when no such compensation has been made, or terms of service secured to their owners?"[38] Bates was similarly aware that in the pre-emancipation incidents involving the liberation of slaves transported in the American vessels *Comet* and *Encomium* and "thrown by stress of weather on the Bahama Islands," the American claim for financial redress "was allowed and paid."[39]

Though *per force,* speculative, and uncertain, it is not unlikely that this stark difference in the treatment of American slave owners as compared to their Bahamian counterparts might have struck Umpire Bates as unjust and warranting correction. The same circumstances, of course, also applied to the cases of the *Enterprize* and the *Hermosa.* The extent, if any, to which such considerations of "fairness" directly or indirectly influenced his judgments will never be known. What is clear is that the outcome was a fairly expensive one for the UK Treasury. Of the total monetary compensation of $329,734 made under the convention to American claimants, some $175,330 went to satisfy the slave-owning interests of those who had suffered financial loss from the liberation of the human 'cargo' aboard those three vessels.[40] It goes without saying that those who had been enslaved received nothing.

It is of relevance to note in this context that especially in recent years the manifest historical injustice surrounding slavery and the slave trade, and the manner of their abolition, has come under increasingly critical scrutiny. A very active international reparations movement has emerged in which the independent Caribbean states, including the Bahamas, have played an influential role and which is now gaining increasing political and diplomatic traction. This seeks reconciliation, truth, and justice from the states which engaged in slavery and the slave trade and recompense for the victims of slavery and their descendants.[41]

Whatever view one adopts as to the conduct of Joshua Bates in this context, it is beyond doubt that he was no natural jurist.[42] After his labors in the various arbitrations which came before him had come to an end, he returned to his life as a highly successful financier. It is perhaps best that he be remembered for his distinction in that sphere and as a generous benefactor of the Boston Public Library. Bates Hall, the ornate reading room in its McKim Building, is named in his honor.[43]

Notwithstanding the efforts of scholars such as Kerr-Ritchie,[44] relatively little is known of the lives of those enslaved persons on the *Creole* who identified an opportunity to find freedom and seized it; even less about their companions who secured their liberty as a result of that mutiny of November 1841. We have seen in this study how their actions—and those of the British colonial authorities in Nassau—caused both outrage and alarm principally among southern interests in the United States. Those same events, however, also helped—at least for a period—to energize the American abolitionist movement. No one used the vivid imagery of this notable case of self-emancipation more often or to greater effect than Frederick Douglass, "who spoke or wrote about Madison Washington a number of times from 1845 to 1861."[45] Indeed, his only work of fiction, the novella *The Heroic Slave*,[46] revolves around the mutiny and especially the figure of Madison Washington. As noted elsewhere, this "has emerged as a major text in Douglass's canon, a novella that continues to engage readers with its compelling vision of reform, black revolution, and the quest for human freedom" (see fig. 10).[47]

As to the brig *Creole*, her life was destined to be a short one. Less than a year after the mutiny in the Bahamian archipelago, she found herself in Funchal Bay in the Portuguese island of Madeira, located north of the Canary Islands and approximately 320 miles west of Morocco. On 24 October 1842, a southerly wind stiffened to hurricane force. As one newspaper was later to report, six vessels were at anchor near Forte de São José da Pontinha when the storm struck "the sea breaking over them with terrific fury; and the wind being dead into the bay, rendered it impossible for them to escape, by making sail and made destruction certain if their anchors dragged."[48] Such was to be the fate of the *Creole*. In a letter to *The Times* of London, a resident of Madeira wrote, "On my arrival at the Pontinha the object of alarm was too clearly marked. The Creole had dragged her anchor, and been driven on shore. In a few seconds she had become a wreck; her keel forced in, her hull broken, and the waves now sporting between the decks which had too often rung with the cries—perhaps, cries to Heaven for vengeance—of imprisoned slaves."[49] Though the wind and waves carried "her bowsprit over the wall of the Sardinian Consul's garden," the seamanship of the mate and "the providence of God" saved the crew.[50]

In 1975, Jones wrote that "[t]he *Creole* revolt should not be ignored."[51]

This study reinforces that view and suggests that it should continue to attract scholarly attention, not least among public international lawyers, and to receive periodic and critical reassessment. More generally, and as Jervey and Huber have advocated, "[i]t rightly deserves a significant place in the struggle over slavery."[52]

Opinion of the Law Officers of the Crown, 29 January 1842

My Lord,

We are honoured with your Lordship's Commands signified in Mr Hope's letter of the 6th Instant, stating that he was directed to transmit to us the Copy of a Despatch and its Enclosures from the Governor of the Bahamas reporting the arrival at the Port of Nassau of an American Brig, the *Creole* with Slaves on board, a portion of whom are stated to have risen upon the Crew during their passage from one Port in America to another, and after murdering a Passenger to have compelled the Crew to carry the Vessel into a Port of the Bahamas. That Sir Francis Cockburn likewise reports the proceedings which took place in this Case subsequently to the arrival of the Vessel off Nassau.

And your Lordship is pleased to request that We would at as early a period as possible report our joint opinion upon the following points.

1st   Whether, the Evidence or the Statements contained in the accompanying Documents justify the conclusion, or the belief that the persons by whom the imputed offences on board the *Creole* are said to have been committed, are in respect of those offences amenable to the Court of the Commissioners constituted at the Bahama Islands under the Statute 46 Geo. 3rd C.54 or to any other Court of Justice in that Colony, or in any other part of the Queen's Dominions.

2nd   Whether the before-mentioned persons are in respect of those offences answerable to the Courts of Criminal Justice within the United States of America, and if so whether the Jurisdiction of those Courts is concurrent with or exclusive of the Courts mentioned in the preceding query.

3rd   Whether according to the Law and practice of Civilized Nations Her Majesty's Government are bound on the demand of the Government of the United States of America to deliver up the persons in question or any of them to that Government to be tried within the United States for their before-mentioned offences, and whether the Municipal Law of England opposes any obstacle to such a delivery up of those persons or any of them to the American Government for that purpose, and whether according to the Law and practice of Civilized Nations, Her Majesty's Government have a discretion on the subject and may refuse (should they think it right to do so) to deliver up the persons in question or any of them.

4th   Whether the Conduct of the Governor of the Bahama Islands and of the persons acting there under his authority as explained in the accompanying Documents was in any (and if any in what) respect at variance with the Law and practice of Civilized Nations or the Municipal Law of this Kingdom.

5th   Whether the principles of Law asserted by the Consul for the United States in his Letter to the Governor 14th November 1841, are just and well founded, and if not, then in what respect and to what extent are those principles erroneous.

6th   Whether the Officers of Customs at the Port of Nassau could lawfully grant to the *Creole* a clearance, and the Ship papers necessary to enable her to leave that Port on her return to the United States; she having on board Slaves, or persons, who in the United States would be regarded and dealt with as Slaves, and if so, whether it would or would not be the duty of such Officers of Customs to ascertain whether such Slaves were about so to return to the United States of their own free and unbiassed Will.

In obedience to your Lordship's Commands We have attentively perused the Despatch of the Governor of the Bahamas, together with its Enclosures, and with respect to the several points upon which our opinion is requested have the honour to report as follows.

1st   We are of opinion that neither the Evidence nor the Statements in the accompanying Documents justify the conclusion or the belief that the persons by whom the imputed offences on board the *Creole* are said to have been committed are in respect of those offences amenable to the Court of the Commissioners constituted at the Bahama Islands under the Statute 46 Geo.3, C.54 or to any other Court of Justice in that Colony or other part of the Queen's Dominions.

It appears to us that the Act of the Negroes in compelling by violence the Crew of the *Creole* to alter her course and take her into a British Port does not either by the General Law of Nations or by the Municipal Law of this Country amount to the Crime of Piracy, and therefore that it is not cognizable by any English Tribunal.

We think there can be little doubt that any Tribunal before which the parties should be brought to trial would come to the conclusion that the intent and object of the Slaves was not that of General Plunder upon the High Seas, or of changing the Property of the Ship, and of converting it to their own use, but that the Acts of which they were guilty were committed with the sole object of compelling the Crew to take them in the Vessel to some Port where they might obtain their Freedom, and we think that the Act of the Slaves committed with such intent and object does not amount to piracy. They may be chargeable with the Crime of Murder, but as they are not British Subjects and the Crime was not committed on board a British Vessel they cannot be tried by a British Tribunal for the Offence.

2nd   And taking this view of the offence we think that having been committed by Persons subject to the American Law on board an American Ship, against the Persons of American Citizens it is exclusively cognizable by the Criminal Tribunals of the United States.

The Justice of each Nation ought to be confined to the Punishment of Crimes committed within its own Territories or by its own Subjects, unless in the case of Pirates and others, who attack and injure all Nations, and who on account of the quality of their Crimes are regarded by the Law of Nations as the Enemies of the Human Race.

3rd   It is the practice of some States to deliver up persons charged with Crimes who have taken refuge or been found within their Dominions on Demand of the Government of which the alleged Criminals are Subjects, but such practice does not universally, or even generally prevail, nor is there any Rule of the Law of Nations rendering it imperative on an Independent State to give up persons residing or taking refuge within its Territory. The mutual surrender of Criminals is indeed sometimes stipulated for by Treaty, but as there is not at present any subsisting Treaty to that effect with the United States of America, we think that Her Majesty's Government is not bound on the Demand of the Government of the United States to deliver up the persons in question or any of them to that Government to be tried within the United States.

4th   We are of opinion that the conduct of the Governor of the Bahama Islands and of the persons acting there under his Authority as explained in the accompanying Documents was not in any respect at variance with the Law and practice of Civilized Nations or of the Municipal Law of this Kingdom.

5th   With respect to the American Consul's Letter, it appears to be written under a misapprehension of the facts. The Slaves were not liberated by the British Authorities nor does it appear that any Control was exercised by them, in this respect over the Crew of the Ship.

6th   We think that the Officers of the Customs might lawfully grant a clearance to the *Creole* to return to the United States and that it was no part of the duty of the Officers of the Customs to ascertain whether the Slaves were returning to America of their own free will or otherwise.

It remains however to be considered whether if Her Majesty's Government should in their judgment deem it to be just and proper to comply with a requisition of the American Government to deliver up the parties to be tried by the Tribunals of the Country, the Municipal Law of England opposes any obstacle to their being delivered over to the

Authorities of the United States for that purpose and we think it right to state to your Lordship that this is a question on which we have felt very considerable difficulty.

The Writers on International Law[1] although they differ as to the extent and binding nature of the obligation, all appear to treat the delivery up of Criminals to the State to which they belong for trial as a recognized and ordinary practice of Civilized Nations, and there are to be found authorities in our English Law Books and the dicta of some of the eminent and learned of our Judges in favour of the exercise of such a power in the Magistrates and Executive Government of the Country. In some of the British Dominions abroad it appears to have been constantly exercised down to the present time and the legality of the practice was sanctioned by a very elaborate and learned Judgment of the Chief Justice of the King's Bench at Montreal in 1827, and has also been supported by the opinion of one of the most eminent of the Lawyers of the United States.[2]

In this Country however an opinion has certainly for many years prevailed and been acted upon that there was no authority in the State which could legally exercise such a power; the opinions of successive Law Officers to that effect have repeatedly been reported to the Government and we apprehend that answers have been given in accordance with such opinions to the demands of Foreign States for the restitution of Criminals who have taken refuge here. This opinion appears to have obtained also the sanction of the Legislature, and we find that after the treaty with America in 1794 and with France and her Allies at the peace of Amiens in 1802, in both of which Treaties there was a stipulation for the mutual surrender by the respective Governments of Persons charged with the Commission of certain heinous offences, it was thought necessary to provide by Act of Parliament for the carrying those stipulations into effect, and for vesting in the Executive Government and in the Magistrates the necessary power for that purpose. These Acts of Parliament were temporary and confined in their operation to the performance of the particular Treaties, and the stipulations referred to have not we believe been renewed in any subsequent Treaty and are not now in force.[3]

We find also that some of the Judges in the American Courts have pronounced opinions unfavourable to the legal existence of such a power and we are informed that the Government of the United States and several of the States comprising the Union professing to act upon the principle of English Law have declared their inability to assist in delivering up to the British Authorities fugitive Criminals from this Country who have taken refuge there.[4]

The Acts of Parliament above referred to although not conclusive upon the point appear to us to be in the nature of a legislative declaration against the existence of such a power independent of the Statute Law and after a most minute investigation of the various conflicting authorities and an anxious consideration of this important subject we feel bound to report to Your Lordship in the absence of any judicial decision on the point in our Courts that in our Judgment the British Government cannot legally direct the delivery up of the persons now in custody in the Bahamas to the Authorities of the United States.

In giving this answer we of course assume that there is no local Law affecting the Bahamas which gives to the Government or the Magistrates in the Colony any peculiar powers in this respect.

We have the honour to be etc.

J. Dodson
Fred. Pollock W. W. Follett

The Rt. Hon. Lord Stanley

Source: National Archives, London, FO 83/2350; A. D. McNair, *International Law Opinions,* vol. 2 (Cambridge University Press, 1956): pp. 85–88.

Case of the *Creole*—Note of the Judgment of the Vice-Admiralty Court of the Bahamas, 16 April 1842

The papers relating to the April 1842 Special Session of the Vice-Admiralty Court are missing from the collections of both the Supreme Court of the Bahamas and the Bahamian National Archives in Nassau. The note of judgment was also published in the 20 April 1842 issue of the Gazette. *Unfortunately, the collection of* Gazettes *held by the Archives in both Nassau and London commence only in the 1890s. Fortunately, the text was reproduced in full in* The Daily Atlas *of Boston, Massachusetts on 28 May 1842 and that which appears below is taken from this source. The text is attributed to the then Chief Justice of the Bahamas.*

CASE OF THE CREOLE

That whether the circumstances under which the homicide alleged to have been committed on board the Creole, when she was taken possession of by the slaves, constituted the crime of murder or not, the Court could not inquire, as no British Court could try a foreigner for an offence committed against another foreigner on the high seas, except for the crime of piracy; for pirates, being deemed enemies of all mankind, could be tried by any nation having competent tribunals for the purpose.

That piracy consists of such robbery or depredation on the high seas, as if it had been committed on shore, would have amounted to felony—or in other words, larceny committed on the sea. That larceny consists in the taking and conveying away the property of another with the intention of defrauding the owner of it, and of converting it to the use of the taker; that there must therefore be proved the *animus furandi* or original intention of stealing, and the *lucri causa* or intention of defrauding the owner of it, and applying it to the profit of the thief,—that if, for example, a man takes a horse from a stable and rides it a certain distance and then abandons it, this is no larceny, because he did not take the horse with the intention of stealing it, but merely for the purpose of conveyance, and did not subsequently convert it to his own use.

That nothing can be more clear than that the laws of one country or state cannot justly bind the subjects of another independent country or state, and that therefore if the subjects of the one are captured and held in bondage by the subjects of the other, such persons have a natural and indefeasible right to recover their liberty when they have the power of doing so. The slaves on board the Creole were thus situated, and could only regain their liberty by taking temporary possession of the vessel, and having so taken possession of her, it appears by facts which have come to our knowledge, and by the examinations which have been taken, that they intended to make no farther use of her than to convey themselves to a British settlement to place themselves under the protection of the British laws; that there being then no original intention of stealing, and no ultimate design of depriving the owners of their vessel, or of converting her *lucri causa,* to their own use, this would not have amounted to a larceny on shore, and consequently not to a piracy at sea.

That the American consul having stated that he had been unable to obtain any evidence against the prisoners from the persons now resident in Nassau who were on board at the time the Creole was taken possession of by the slaves, and having therefore requested that the trial might be postponed till he could communicate with his Government, in order to move it to send to Nassau the crew and passengers of the Creole, the Court had read attentively the examinations of the said crew and passengers, upon which the consul grounded this application, and wishing to comply with any request made by that gentleman, would certainly have granted it, could they have entertained any reasonable supposition that credible evidence could be brought to convict the prisoners of piracy, but that in only one of the examinations, that of Mr Lightner, did there appear any evidence whatever of any piratical proceeding on the part of the slaves.

Mr Lightner states that he had seen them break open a trunk, and take out some money, and take also wearing apparel; but in the first place that examination was taken *ex parte* by the then American consul, neither in the presence of a British magistrate, nor in the presence of the prisoners; that Mr Lightner states only that some of the negroes did this, without attempting to lay the charge to any one of the prisoners or those concerned in the capture of the vessel; and thirdly, that the examinant was one who signed the protest of the 7th of December last, at New Orleans, a protest notorious to every one in this community, for its gross misstatements of facts; that under these circumstances, as it appeared to the Court that it was very doubtful whether the witnesses named by the consul would be sent here at all, and that even if they were the prisoners could not be convicted of piracy, however reluctant the commissioners were to refuse compliance with that gentleman's wishes, they did not think they could with any degree of justice consent to commit the prisoners to any farther confinement, and must therefore order them to be discharged.

The *Creole* (USA v. Great Britain), Award by the Umpire, 9 January 1855

London, 9th January 1855

The umpire reports that this claim has grown out of the following circumstances:—

The American brig "Creole," Captain Ensor, sailed from Hampton Roads, in the State of Virginia, on the 27th of October, 1841, having on board 135 slaves bound for New Orleans. On the 7th November, at 9 o'clock in the evening, a portion of the slaves rose against the officers, crew and passengers, wounding severely the captain, the chief mate and two of the crew, and murdering one of the passengers. The mutineers having got complete possession of the vessel, ordered the mate under threat of instant death should he disobey or deceive them, to steer for Nassau in the Island of New Providence, where the brig arrived on the 9th November, 1841. The American Consul was apprised of the situation of the vessel; he requested the Governor to take measures to prevent the escape of the slaves, and to have the murderers secured. The Consul received reply from the Governor, stating, that under the circumstances he would comply with the request. The Consul went on board the brig, placed the mate in command in place of the disabled master, and found the slaves all quiet. About noon, twenty African soldiers with an African sergeant and corporal, commanded by a white officer, came on board, the officer was introduced by the Consul to the mate as commanding officer of the vessel. The Consul on returning to the shore was summoned to attend the Governor and Council who were in Session, who informed the Consul that they had come to the following decision:—

"1st   That the Courts of Law have no jurisdiction over the alleged offences."

"2nd   That as an information had been lodged before the Governor, charging that the crime of murder had been committed on board said vessel while on the high seas, it was expedient that the parties implicated in so grave a charge, should not be allowed to go at large, and that an investigation ought therefore to be made into the charges, and examinations taken on oath; when, if it should appear that the original information was correct, and that a murder had actually been committed, that all the parties implicated in such crime or other acts of violence, should be detained here until reference could be made to the Secretary of State, to ascertain whether the parties should be delivered over to The United States' Government, if not, how otherwise to dispose of them."

"3rd   That as soon as such examination should be taken, all persons on board the 'Creole' not implicated in any of the offences alleged to have been committed on board that vessel, must be released from further restraint."

Then two magistrates were sent on board. The American Consul went also. The examination was commenced on Tuesday the 9th and was continued on Wednesday the 10th, and then postponed until Friday, on account of the illness of Captain Ensor. On Friday morning it was abruptly and without any explanation terminated. On the same day, a large number of boats assembled near the "Creole" filled with coloured persons armed with bludgeons. They were under the immediate command of the pilot who took the vessel into the port,—who was an officer of the Government—and a coloured man. A sloop or larger launch was also towed from the shore and anchored near the brig; the sloop was filled with men armed with clubs, and clubs were passed from her to the persons in the boats; a vast concourse of people were collected on shore opposite the brig. During the whole time the officers of the Government were on board, they encouraged the insubordination of the slaves. The Americans in port determined to unite and furnish the necessary aid to forward the vessel and negroes to New Orleans. The Consul and the officers and crews of two other American vessels in fact combined with the officers, men and passengers of the "Creole," to effect this. They were to conduct her first to Indian Quay, Florida, where there was a vessel of war of The United States. On Friday morning, the Consul was informed that attempts would be made to liberate the slaves by force, and from the mate he received information of the threatening state of things. The result was, the Attorney-General and other officers went on board the "Creole"; the slaves identified as on board the vessel concerned in the mutiny were sent on shore, and the residue of the slaves were called on deck by direction of the Attorney-General, who addressed them in the following terms:—"My friends" or "My men, you have been detained a short time on board the 'Creole' for the purpose of ascertaining what individuals were concerned in the murder. They have been identified and will be detained. The rest of you are free and at liberty to go on shore, and wherever you please." The liberated slaves assisted by the magistrates, were then taken on board the boats, and when landed, were conducted by a vast assemblage to the Superintendent of Police, by whom their names were registered. They were thus forcibly taken from the custody of the master of the "Creole," and lost to the claimants.

I need not refer to authorities to shew that slavery, however odious and contrary to the principles of justice and humanity, may be established by law in any country, and, having been so established in many countries, it cannot be contrary to the law of nations. The "Creole" was on a voyage sanctioned and protected by the laws of The United States, and by the law of nations; her right to navigate the ocean could not be questioned, and, as growing out of that right, the right to seek shelter, or enter the ports of a friendly power in case of distress or any unavoidable necessity.

A vessel navigating the ocean, carries with her the laws of her own country, so far as relates to the persons and property on board, and to a certain extent even in the ports of the foreign nations she may visit. Now this being the state of the law of nations, what were the duties of the authorities at Nassau, in regard to the "Creole"? It is submitted the mutineers could not be tried by the courts of that Island, the crime having been committed on the high seas. All that the authorities could lawfully do was to comply with the request of the American Consul, and keep the mutineers in custody until a conveyance could be found for sending them to The United States. The other slaves being perfectly quiet and under the command of the captain and owners, and on board an American ship, the authorities should have seen that they were protected by the laws of nations, their rights under which cannot be abrogated or varied either by the Emancipation Act or any other Act of the British Parliament. Blackstone, 4th volume, speaking of the law of nations, states "Whenever any question arises, which is properly the object of its jurisdiction, such law is here adopted in its full extent by the common law."

The municipal law of England cannot authorize a magistrate to violate the law of nations, by invading with an armed force the vessel of a friendly nation that has committed no offence, and forcibly dissolving the relations which, by the laws of his country, the captain is bound to preserve and enforce on board. These rights, sanctioned by the law of nations, viz., the right to navigate the ocean and to seek shelter in case of distress or other unavoidable circumstances, and to retain over the ship, her cargo, and passengers, the laws of her own country, must be respected by all nations, for no independent nation would submit to their violation.

Having read all the authorities referred to in the arguments on both sides. I have come to the conclusion that the conduct of the authorities at Nassau was in violation of the established law of nations, and that the claimants are justly entitled to compensation for their losses; I therefore award to the undermentioned parties, their assigns, or their legal representatives, the sums set opposite their names, on the 15th January, 1855, viz.:

To Edward Lockett	Twenty-two thousand two hundred and fifty dollars
To John Pemberton Liquidator of the Merchant's Insurance Company of New Orleans	Twelve thousand four hundred and sixty dollars

To John Hagan	Eight thousand dollars
To William H Goodwin, for self and Thomas Mc Cargo	Twenty-three thousand one hundred and forty dollars
To G. H. Apperson and Sherman Johnson	Twenty thousand four hundred and seventy dollars
To P. Rotchford	Two thousand one hundred and thirty-six dollars
To John Pemberton, Liquidator of the Merchant's Insurance Company of New Orleans	Sixteen thousand dollars
To James Andrews	Five thousand eight hundred and seventy-four dollars

making together one hundred and ten thousand three hundred and thirty dollars.

JOSHUA BATES, *Umpire.*

Source: Reproduced in, E. Hornby (ed.), *Report of the Proceedings of the Mixed Commission on Private Claims* (London: Harrison and Sons, 1856): pp. 389–393.

The *Maria Luz* (Peru v. Japan), Award of the Emperor of Russia, May 1875

We, Alexander II, by the grace of God, Emperor of all the Russias.

In compliance with the request which has been made to us by the governments of Japan and Peru, contained in a protocol drawn up with common consent at Tokei by the plenipotentiaries of the two governments on the 13th and 25th of June, 1873, corresponding to the 25th day of the 6th month of the 6th year of Meiji, we have agreed to examine the difference pending between the two governments in connection with the stay of the ship *"Maria Luz,"* in the port of Kanagawa, and particularly the claim of the Peruvian government, tending to render the Japanese government responsible for all the consequences arising out of the action of the Japanese authorities with respect to the "Maria Luz," her crew and passengers, at the time of the stay of that ship at Kanagawa, and we have consented to take upon ourselves the task of pronouncing a sentence of arbitration which shall be definitive and obligatory for both parties, and as to which no objection, explanation, or delay whatever shall be made.

Having, consequently, maturely weighed the considerations and conclusions of the juris consults, and of the competent persons, charged to study the affair, from the documents and statements which have been transmitted to us in conformity with the above mentioned protocol—

We have arrived at the conviction, that in proceeding as it did with regard to the "Maria Luz," her crew and passengers, the Japanese government acted in good faith (*bona fide*) in virtue of its own laws and customs, without infringing the general prescriptions of the law of nations, or the stipulations of particular treaties.

That therefore it cannot be reproached for a willful want of respect, or for any malevolent intention, toward the Peruvian government or its citizens.

That the various kinds of opinions provoked by this incident may inspire governments who have no special treaties with Japan, with the desire to make reciprocal international relations more precise, in order to avoid in the future every similar misunderstanding; for they cannot, in the absence of formal stipulations, cause to be placed upon the Japanese government the responsibility of action which it has not wittingly provoked, and of measures which are in conformity with its own legislation.

Consequently we have not found sufficient grounds for recognizing, as irregular, the acts of the Japanese authorities in the affair of the ship "Maria Luz"; and attributing the losses sustained to an unfortunate combination of circumstances,

We pronounce the following sentence of arbitration:

The government of Japan is not responsible for the consequences which were produced by the stay of the Peruvian ship "Maria Luz" in the port of Kanagawa.

In faith whereof we have signed the present sentence, and have caused our imperial seal to be affixed thereto.

Done at Ems the 17th (29th) May, 1875.

(The original is signed by the hand of His Majesty the Emperor.)

(SEAL)   ALEXANDER

For true copy:
The acting minister for foreign affairs   BARON JOMINI

Source: This is the translation of the Award provided to the US Department of State by its legation in St. Petersburg. See Schuyler to Fish, 22 June 1875, in *Executive Documents Printed by Order of the House of Representatives 1875–76,* vol. 2 (Washington, DC: Government Printing Office, Washington, 1876): pp. 1066–67. For the French original, see *Annuaire de l'Institut de Droit International,* vol. 1 (1877): pp. 353–54.

Notes

Introduction

1. See, generally, Williams, *Capitalism and Slavery.*

2. See Watson, *Slave Law in the Americas.*

3. See Bush, "The British Constitution and the Creation of Slavery in America."

4. Roberts-Wray, *Commonwealth and Colonial Law*, p. 540. In colonies conquered from or ceded by foreign powers, the law in force at the time of transfer of sovereignty remained in force. See *id.*, at pp. 541–42.

5. *Id.*, p. 151.

6. *Supra* note 2, p. 63.

7. 2 Salk, 666.

8. 1 Lofft 499, at p. 510. For the position in the law of Scotland, see *Knight* v. *Wedderburn* (1778), Hailes's Decisions, 776. See also Cairns, "After *Somerset:* The Scottish Experience," pp. 291–312.

9. Schafer, *Slavery, the Civil Law, and the Supreme Court of Louisiana*, pp. 26–27.

10. McNair, *International Law Opinions*, vol. 2, at pp. 77–78.

11. Wish, "American Slave Insurrections before 1861," p. 299, at p. 300. See also Taylor, *If We Must Die: Shipboard Insurrections in the Era of the Atlantic Slave Trade.*

12. See Kelley, *American Slavers: Merchants, Mariners, and the Trans-Atlantic Commerce in Captives, 1644–1865*, at p. 7.

13. For a summary see, e.g., Taylor, *supra* note 11, at pp. 151–56. For a detailed account, see Jones, *Mutiny on the Amistad: The Saga of a Slave Revolt and its Impact on American Abolition, Law and Diplomacy.* The 1997 film *Amistad,* directed by Steven Spielberg, did much to embed this event into popular culture. However, "the story of the *Creole* and the incredible heroism that it once represented remain largely hidden from popular view." See Finkenbine, "The Symbolism of Slave Mutiny: Black Abolitionist Responses to the *Amistad* and *Creole* Incidents," p. 233, at p. 248.

14. See *United States v. Libellants and Claimants of the Schooner Amistad, Her Tackle, Apparel, and Furniture, Together with Her Cargo, and the Africans Mentioned and Described in the Several Libels and Claims,* 40 US 518 (1841).

15. Fox to Palmerston, 9 March 1841 (1841–1842), *BFSP,* vol. 30, p. 1140.

16. *Id.*

17. For a brief summary, see Taylor, *supra* note 11, at pp. 156–59.

18. *Supra* note 14, at p. 593.

19. *Id.*

20. J. C., "Case of the Creole," p. 79, at p. 90. For an explanation by the editors of the use of the initials of contributors see *id.*, at p. 191.

21. This trade between slave states in America (in this instance between Virginia and Louisiana) was prohibited in law only in the course of the Civil War. That trade was extensive. One commentator has remarked: "By 1841 hundreds of vessels, their holds full of slaves, had made the same journey the *Creole* was making around the south eastern coast of North America, from Virginia, along the Gulf Cost, and on to New Orleans; as would, in succeeding years, hundreds more." See Johnson, "White Lies: Human Property and Domestic Slavery Aboard the Slave Ship *Creole,*" p. 237, at p. 239.

22. *McCargo v. Merchants Insurance Company of New Orleans—Lockett v. The Same—Application for a Re-hearing,* 10 Rob (LA) 349 (1845), at p. 351.

1. Flight to Freedom

1. A brig was a then-common sailing vessel characterized by two square-rigged masts.

2. See Kerr-Ritchie, *Rebellious Passage: The Creole Revolt and America's Coastal Slave Trade,* at pp. 78–81.

3. See *id.*, at pp. 81–82.

4. *Id.*, p. 77. In the subsequent case of *McCargo v. New Orleans Insurance Co.* 10 Rob (LA) 202 (1845), at p. 260, counsel for the company stated that it was 157 and 25/95th tons.

5. See Jervey and Huber, "The *Creole* Affair," p. 196, at p. 196.

6. There is some dispute in the literature as to the exact number of enslaved persons on board. The diplomatic record invariably utilizes the 135 total. Kerr-Ritchie provides an alternative estimate of 139. See *supra* note 2, at p. 91. Kerr-Ritchie's appendix 3, *id.*, at pp. 295–302, constitutes a valuable resource on each individual concerned. This reveals that the enslaved were shipped by, or on behalf of, various parties, chief among them Thomas McCargo, Robert Lumpkin, and George W. Apperson.

7. The American coastal slave trade was an exception to the central thrust of the 2 March 1807 Act to prohibit the importation of Slaves into any port or place within the Jurisdiction of the United States, 2 Stat. 426 (1807). This had as its focus the international trade in enslaved persons. However, it contained administrative requirements designed to minimize the possibility of abusing this exception. See sections 9 and 10. The coastal

trade was only abolished during the Civil War. On 2 July 1864, the relevant provisions were repealed "and the coastwise slave-trade is prohibited forever." An Act making Appropriations . . . and for other Purposes, 13 Stat. 344 (1864).

8. Vail held that post from 1832 to 1836.

9. Then Lord Palmerston.

10. Reproduced in "Message from the President of the United States with Copies of Correspondence in Relation to the Seizure of Slaves on Board the Brigs 'Encomium' and 'Enterprize,'" 24th Congress, 2d Session, Senate, p. 25, at p. 26. See also Levy, *Freaks of Fortune: The Emerging World of Capitalism and Risk in America,* at pp. 23–24.

11. New Orleans Protest of 7 December 1841, reproduced in "Message from the President of the United States: In Compliance with a Resolution of the Senate, Copies of Correspondence in Relation to the Mutiny on Board the Brig Creole, and the Liberation of the Slaves Who Were Passengers in the Said Vessel," 27th Congress, 2d Session, Senate, January 1842 [hereafter January 1842 Senate Doc.], p. 36, at p. 37.

12. See, e.g., *id.*, at p. 37.

13. *Id.*

14. It is understood that this feature collapsed in 2012 in the aftermath of Hurricane Sandy.

15. *Supra* note 11, p. 37.

16. Various accounts of this revolt exist. See Chadwick, *The Creole Rebellion: The Most Successful Slave Revolt in American History,* at pp. 14–26; and *supra* note 5, at pp. 197–201. The primary and secondary source materials preponderantly point to four as having been particularly influential: viz, Benjamin Johnstone (aka Blacksmith), Elijah Morris, "Doctor" Ruffin, and Madison Washington. All were in their early to mid-twenties. Of these, Madison Washington was to become the best-known to history.

17. Everett, who was close to Secretary of State Webster, was America's top diplomat in the UK from 1841 to 1845. His full title was "envoy extraordinary and minister plenipotentiary" to the Court of St. James. The terms "envoy" and "minister" will be utilized for the purposes of the work. He enjoyed a diverse and stellar career including a period as secretary of state (1852–53).

18. Everett to Aberdeen, 1 March 1842, (1842–1843) *BFSP,* vol. 31, p. 675, at p. 676. As noted at a later stage of this chapter, at least one of the enslaved died subsequently as a result of his wounds.

19. See Dale, *The Modern Commonwealth,* at p. 204. At that time, what are now the Turks and Caicos Islands, situated to the southwest, were functionally part of the colony of the Bahamas. See *id.*, at p. 318.

20. Roberts-Wray, *Commonwealth and Colonial Law,* p. 811.

21. See *id.*, at p. 812.

22. *Id.*, p. 540.

23. See *id.*, at p. 814.

24. See Saunders, "Slave-Owners' Compensation: The Bahamas Colony," p. 45, at p. 47, Table 1.

25. McNair, *International Law Opinions,* vol. 2, p. 77.

26. c.73 (UK). This extended, by paramount force, throughout the Empire with the exception of territories possessed by the East India Company, Ceylon, and Saint Helena.

27. See, generally, the website of the Centre for the Study of the Legacies of British Slavery (www.ucl.ac.uk/lbs/project/details/).

28. *Supra* note 24, p. 51. According to the CPI-based Bank of England inflation calculator this equates to £13,567,485 in June 2023 terms.

29. "Protest—Brig Creole" of 17 November 1841, in January 1842 Senate Doc, *op. cit.*, p. 16, at p. 17. This crew believed "was a very dangerous situation in case of the northwest wind, and a place where vessels never remain." *Id.* On 13 November the vessel was moved "further into the harbor, and out of danger from bad weather." *Id.*, p. 18. This protest, executed in the US Consulate in Nassau is not to be confused with the New Orleans Protest of 7 December 1841 mentioned at note 11 above.

30. See New Orleans Protest, *supra* note 11, at p. 42.

31. See Bacon to Webster, 30 November 1841, in January 1842 Senate Doc, *op. cit.*, at pp. 2–3.

32. See, generally, McKenna, "Cockburn, Sir Francis."

33. Bacon to Cockburn, 9 November 1841, in January 1842 Senate Doc, *op. cit.*, p. 5.

34. Nesbitt to Bacon, 9 November 1841, *id.*

35. See, e.g., *supra* note 2, at pp. 131–32.

36. See, e.g., Bacon to Webster, 17 November 1841, in January 1842 Senate Doc, *op. cit.*, at p. 2.

37. See Moore, *A Digest of International Law,* vol. 2, at pp. 350–51.

38. See, e.g., *The Hermosa* (USA v. Great Britain) XXIX Reports of International Arbitral Awards 50. This incident may well have influenced the choice by the mutineers of the Bahamas as the destination. As Levy, *supra* note 10, informs us at p. 25, "they insisted that they wished to go where Mr Lumpkin's slaves had gone the previous year." Many of the enslaved aboard the *Creole* "came from Robert Lumpkin's infamous Richmond, Virginia, slave pen. Obviously, they knew of the *Hermosa.*" See also, New Orleans Protest, *supra,* note 11, at p. 40. Also of interest in this context is Troutman, "Grapevine in the Slave Market: African American Geopolitical Literacy and the 1841 *Creole* Revolt," p. 203, at pp. 208–10 and pp. 213–14. Bacon, the US Consul, had—like Governor Cockburn—been in post during the *Hermosa* incident of October 1840 and had, no doubt, learned much from that experience.

39. See, e.g., *The Enterprize* (USA v. Great Britain) XXIX Reports of International Arbitral Awards 48.

40. See chapter 4 below.

41. See, generally, *supra* note 10.

42. On the compensation paid see, e.g., "Indemnities for Slaves on Board the Comet and Encomium," 27th Congress, 2d Session, House of Representatives, Doc. No. 242.

43. Colonial Office, Circular Dispatch 25 May 1839. National Archives, London, CO 318/146.

44. Copy of Treasury Minute of 12 April 1839 enclosed with *id.* The same principle is articulated in the Copy of the Treasury Minute of 6 December 1836 which was also enclosed with the Circular Dispatch.

45. See *supra* note 31.

46. Attachment to Nesbitt to Bacon, 9 November 1841, reproduced in January 1842 Senate Doc., pp. 5–6.

47. Bacon to Webster, 30 November 1841, *supra* note 31, p. 3.

48. *Supra* note 2, p. 137.

49. These depositions are reproduced in January 1842 Senate Doc., *supra* note 11, at pp. 28–36. The sworn testimony of Captain Ensor was delayed, due to his medical condition, to 18 November. See *id.*, at p. 30.

50. See, e.g., *supra* note 2, at p. 137.

51. See the written account of events dated 13 November 1841 prepared by the Attorney General and attached to Cockburn to Bacon, 15 November 1841, in January 1842 Senate Doc., *op. cit.*, p. 8, at p. 9.

52. See, e.g., Bacon to Webster, 30 November 1841, reproduced *id.*, p. 2, at p. 4.

53. See Nesbitt to Bacon, 26 November 1841, in *Correspondence with Foreign Powers Not Parties to Conventions Giving Right of Search of Vessels Suspected of the Slave Trade: 1842* (HMSO, London, 1843): p. 144. The record is somewhat confused on the subject of fatalities among the enslaved involved in the mutiny. The New Orleans Protest, *supra* note 11, p. 40 speaks of "two of the Negroes [being] severely wounded by handspikes." Some media reports recorded somewhat higher numbers. On 18 December the *Atlas* of Boston, Mass., under the headline "Mutiny and Murder" reported: "[t]hree of the slaves were killed in the affray, and another died of his wounds after his arrival at Nassau." Nonetheless, it is possible to agree with Levine et al. that "The rebellion was comparatively civil. . . . Taking into account the numbers liberated versus those killed, it was one of the most successful slave revolts in North America." See Levine et al., *The Heroic Slave: A Cultural and Critical Edition*, p. xi.

54. See, e.g., *supra* note 2, at pp. 140–43.

55. Bacon to Cockburn, 12 November 1841, in January 1842 Senate Doc., p. 6. It is clear from the testimony given by Bacon sometime later in the course of litigation before the Supreme Court of Louisiana that the basis for these concerns arose out of conversations on the day with several "respectable" white residents of Nassau. See *McCargo v. New Orleans Insurance Co.*, 10 Rob (LA) 202 (1845), p. 224, at pp. 226–27.

56. Cockburn to Bacon, 12 November 1841, reproduced in *id.*, at p. 7.

57. Bacon to Webster, 30 November 1841, reproduced in *id.*, p. 2, at p. 3. He further informed the Secretary of State that "I immediately communicated this information to the mate and Captain Woodside; and requested the mate to return to the vessel and protest against every act of the attorney general or his party, which should liberate the slaves: I also requested Captain Woodside to accompany him." *Id.*

58. See, e.g., Bacon to Webster, 17 November 1841, reproduced in *id.*, p. 2; New Orleans Protest, *supra* note 11, at pp. 43–44; and Kerr-Ritchie, *op. cit.*, at p. 154. See also Gilmore, *The Confederate Jurist: The Legal Life of Judah P Benjamin,* p. 20, note 51.

59. Bacon to Webster, 30 November 1841, reproduced in January 1842 Senate Doc., *op. cit.*, p. 2, at p. 4.

60. See, e.g., Gilmore, *op. cit.*, at p. 19. Notwithstanding the efforts of several American historians, relatively little is known about those so liberated or, indeed, of those who had participated in the mutiny itself. By way of illustration, no images of those involved have come to the attention of the author and were thus not available for reproduction in this study.

61. See text at note 55, *supra*.

62. *Supra* note 5, p. 202. See also, e.g., Jones, "The Peculiar Institution and National Honor: The Case of the *Creole* Slave Revolt," p. 28, at p. 32. In his testimony in the *McCargo* case in 1845, *supra* note 55, at p. 229, Bacon asserted that, in conversation with the Governor on 12 November, the Governor stated "that he had just been informed that I had attempted to send on board the brig a large amount of arms and ammunition, with some men."

63. See New Orleans Protest, *supra* note 11, at pp. 44–45.

64. *Id.*, p. 45. To a similar effect, see the testimony of Bacon in the *McCargo* case, *supra* note 55, at p. 232.

65. In his 30 November 1841 dispatch to Secretary of State Webster, reproduced in January 1842 Senate Doc, *op. cit.*, p. 2, the US Consul makes passing mention of several American seamen proceeding to the *Creole* at his request. *Id.*, p. 3.

66. In setting out the factual circumstances surrounding this dispute the umpire remarked: "The Americans in port determined to unite and furnish the necessary aid to forward the vessel and negroes to New Orleans. The consul and the officers and crews of two other American vessels had, in fact, united with the officers, men, and passengers of the *Creole* to effect this. They were to conduct her first to Indian Key, Florida, where there was a vessel of war of the United States." *The Creole* (USA v. Great Britain) XXIX Reports of International Arbitral Awards, p. 51, at p. 52. For ease of reference this award is reproduced in full as appendix 3.

67. See, in particular, chapter 4.

68. Reproduced in January 1842 Senate Doc., at pp. 10–16.

69. Bacon to Cockburn, 14 November 1841, *id.*, p. 7.

70. *Id.*

71. *Id.*

72. See *id.*, at pp. 7–8.

73. Cockburn to Bacon, 15 November 1841, in *id.*, at p. 8.

74. *Id.*

75. *Supra* note 51, p. 10.

76. *Id.*

77. *Supra* note 73.

78. [1824–34] All ER 48. On the career of this distinguished relative, see, e.g., Morriss and Cooper, *Cockburn and the British Navy in Transition: Admiral Sir George Cockburn, 1772–1853.*

79. The present-day international law of the sea embodies an extended version of that principle; namely, that "[a]ny slave taking refuge on board any ship, whatever its flag, shall *ipso facto* be free." Art. 99, 1982 United Nations Convention on the Law of the Sea.

2. The Mutineers in Nassau Jail

1. Henry S. Fox (later knighted) was the British "envoy extraordinary and minister plenipotentiary" to the United States 1835–1843.

2. Lord Stanley (later the Earl of Derby) was secretary of state for the colonies (1841–1845). He was subsequently thrice prime minister of the UK.

3. Cockburn to Stanley, 17 November 1841, National Archives, London, CO 23/110.

4. *Id.*

5. *Id.*

6. The Earl of Aberdeen (aka Lord) was foreign secretary (1841–1846). He subsequently served a term as prime minister (1852–1855).

7. Colonial Office to Canning, [?] January 1842, National Archives, London, CO 23/110. Viscount Canning was the then under-secretary of state for foreign affairs. He was requested to make the foreign secretary aware of its contents.

8. Bacon to Webster, 17 November 1842, in "Message from the President of the United States: In Compliance with a Resolution of the Senate, Copies of Correspondence in Relation to the Mutiny on Board the Brig Creole, and the Liberation of the Slaves Who Were Passengers in the Said Vessel," 27th Congress, 2d Session, Senate, January 1842 [hereafter January 1842 Senate Doc.], p. 2.

9. Reproduced at *id.*, pp. 36–46.

10. Jervey and Huber, "The *Creole* Affair," p. 196, at p. 205. See also, e.g., Chadwick, *The "Creole" Rebellion: The Most Successful Slave Revolt in American History,* p. 93.

11. See, e.g., Jones, "The Peculiar Institution and National Honor: The Case of the *Creole* Slave Revolt," p. 28, at pp. 33–34.

12. Vega, "*Creole* Case (1841)," p. 148.

13. Fox to Aberdeen, 28 December 1841 (received 16 January 1842) in *Correspondence with Foreign Powers not Parties to Conventions Giving Right of Search of Vessels Suspected of the Slave Trade: 1842* (HMSO, London, 1843): p. 112.

14. See, e.g., Kerr-Ritchie, *Rebellious Passage: The Creole Revolt and America's Coastal Slave Trade,* p. 173 ("members of Britain's highest court").

15. See, e.g., O'Connell and Riordon, *Opinions on Imperial Constitutional Law*, at vi.

16. For example, the lord advocate and solicitor general of Scotland were rarely, if ever, consulted on such matters.

17. See, e.g., Lobban, "Twiss, Sir Travers (1809–1897)."

18. See, e.g., Rigg, "Pollock, Sir (Jonathan) Frederick, first baronet (1783–1870)."

19. See Hamilton, "Follett, Sir William Webb (1796–1845)."

20. King's Advocate prior to the accession of Victoria to the throne.

21. See, e.g., Boase, "Dodson, Sir John (1780–1858)."

22. See, generally, McNair, *International Law Opinions,* vol. 2, chapter 5 (entitled "Slavery and the Slave Trade").

23. Text reproduced in January 1842 Senate Doc., *op. cit.*, pp. 5–6.

24. "The Case of the Creole," *The Spectator* 15, no. 708 (22 January 1842), p.85, at p. 86.

25. See, e.g., Bantekas, "Criminal Jurisdiction of States under International Law," *Max Planck Encyclopedias of International Law* (online edition), paras. 4–12.

26. By way of contrast, states from the civil law tradition invariably invoke, in addition to territoriality, the nationality principle of prescriptive jurisdiction.

27. See, e.g., Bantekas, *supra* note 25, at paras. 6–8. This rule of customary law is now codified in Art 92(1) of the 1982 United Nations Convention on the Law of the Sea.

28. See also National Archives, London, FO 83/2350.

29. Bantekas, *supra* note 25, para. 9.

30. See, e.g., McNair, *op. cit.*, vol. 1, at p. 265.

31. The definition of piracy in the Law of Nations is now codified in Art. 101 of the 1982 United Nations Convention on the Law of the Sea. Its approach, in turn, was borrowed from Art. 15 of the 1958 United Nations Convention on the High Seas. It reads as follows: "Piracy consists of any of the following acts: (1) Any illegal acts of violence, detention or any act of depredation, committed for private ends by the crew or the passengers of a private ship or a private aircraft, and directed: (a) On the high seas, against another ship or aircraft, or against persons or property on board such ship or aircraft; (b) Against a ship, aircraft, persons or property in a place outside the jurisdiction of any State; (2) Any act of voluntary participation in the operation of a ship or of an aircraft with knowledge of facts making it a pirate ship or aircraft; (3) Any act of inciting or of intentionally facilitating an act described in subparagraph 1 or subparagraph 2 of this article." The preparatory work for this formulation was undertaken by the influential International Law Commission. It identified six "controversial points as to the essential features of piracy." In that most

relevant to the facts of the *Creole* incident it concluded: "Acts committed on board a ship by the crew or passengers and directed against the ship itself, or against persons or property, on the ship, cannot be regarded as acts of piracy." *Yearbook of the International Law Commission,* vol. 2 (1956): p. 282. This approach "tallies with the opinion of most writers. Even where the purpose of the mutineers is to seize the ship, their acts do not constitute acts of piracy." *Id.*

32. McNair, *op. cit.*, vol. 1, p. 265.

33. *Supra* note 3.

34. See generally, e.g., Gilbert, *Transnational Fugitive Offenders in International Law: Extradition and Other Mechanisms.*

35. See, e.g., *id.,* at pp. 47–48.

36. For example, in relation to the incident in Bermuda concerning the *Enterprize* considered in the previous chapter. See also chapter 4 below.

37. Stanley to Cockburn, 31 January 1842, National Archives, London, CO 24/22. It is of relevance to note that the Queen's Advocate adopted a nearly identical view in April 1842 concerning an enslaved person who had been aboard a French vessel in St John's Harbor in the British colony of Antigua. See, Dodson to Aberdeen, 14 April 1842, National Archives, London, FO 83/2350.

38. Bacon to Cockburn, 14 November 1841, reproduced in January 1842 Senate Doc.; *supra* note 8, at pp. 7–8.

39. *Supra* note 37.

40. See, e.g., "Mutiny and Murder," *The Observer,* 16 January 1842, p. 4, and "America—Slavery—The Rights of Man," *The Observer,* 17 January 1842, p. 2.

41. See "The Creole Mutiny," *Times,* 21 January 1842, p. 3.

42. See HL Deb 14 February 1842, vol. 60, cc. 317–327. For media coverage of this debate, see, e.g., *Times,* 16 February 1842, p. 13. See also, Jones, *supra* note 11, at p. 40.

43. All held or had previously held high judicial office.

44. Aberdeen to Everett, 18 April 1842, reproduced *supra* note 13, p. 193, at p. 194.

45. See, generally, chapter 3 below.

46. Quoted by Jervey and Huber, *supra* note 10, at p. 205. See also *supra* note 14, at p. 175.

47. See, generally, January 1842 Senate Doc., *op. cit.* In a note of 18 January 1842, Secretary of State Webster had informed President Tyler that "no application has been made to the Department of State by the owners or underwriters, requesting the interference of this Government, but that, on the receipt of the communications from the Consul, and the protests, the Secretary was directed to prepare a despatch for the American minister in London, which will be forwarded without unnecessary delay." Reproduced in *id.*, p. 1.

48. See Jay, *The Creole Case and Mr. Webster's Despatch,* at p. 5.

49. Fox to Aberdeen, 25 February 1842 (received 26 March), reproduced in *supra* note 13, p. 160. This version misprints the year as 1824.

50. Webster to Everett, 29 January 1842, reproduced in *id.*, p. 161, at p. 161.

51. *Id.*, p. 163.

52. *Id.*, p. 162.

53. *Id.*, p. 164.

54. Everett to Aberdeen, 1 March 1842, reproduced in *id.*, at p. 115 *et seq.*

55. See Aberdeen to Everett, 18 April 1842, reproduced in *id.*, at p. 193 *et seq.*

56. *Supra* note 37.

57. *Id.*

58. Cockburn to Darling, 30 March 1842, National Archives, London, CO 23/112.

59. Darling to Cockburn, 31 March 1842, *id.*

60. Cockburn to Darling, 1 April 1842, *id.*

61. The Governor considered it very doubtful that the court would agree to a postponement of the proceedings. See Cockburn to Stanley, 5 April 1842, *id.*

62. Darling to Cockburn, 2 April 1842, *id.*

63. Darling to Webster, 16 April 1842, US National Archives, Washington, DC, "Despatches from United States Consuls in Nassau, New Providence Island 1821–1906," vol. 6, January 4, 1842–December 28, 1846; Microcopy No T-475, Roll 6, Image 46 *et seq.*

64. *Supra* note 14, p. 83.

65. *Supra* note 63.

66. See *id.*

67. Cockburn to Stanley, 17 April 1842 (received 10 May 1842), National Archives, London, CO 23/112.

68. See *id.*

69. *Id.*

70. "From Nassau—The Creole Negroes Set at Liberty," *The Weekly Ohio State Journal*, 18 May 1842, p. 2. See also "The Creole Negroes," *Times*, 18 May 1842, p. 3.

71. Other variants were utilized by the press. For example, "The seventeen were accordingly discharged under proclamation, with the admonition to behave themselves as good subjects of Her Majesty's Government, as they had, by a signal interposition of Divine Providence, been liberated from slavery." "The Creole Case," *Daily Atlas*, 7 May 1842, p. 2.

72. The papers relating to the April 1842 Special Session of the Vice-Admiralty Court are missing from the collection held by the Bahamian National Archives in Nassau. Email from the Director of Archives of 14 March 2022 on file with the author.

73. It was reproduced in the 20 April 1842 issue. Unfortunately, the collection of *Gazettes* held by the archives in Nassau and London commence only in the 1890s.

74. Fortunately, the full text of the note of judgment was reproduced by the *Daily Atlas*, 28 May 1842, at p. 2. It is this version which has been utilized in the appendix.

75. It was an obvious relief to London that this had taken the form of a judicial and not executive act. Of interest in this regard is Colonial Office to Canning, 21 May 1842,

National Archives, London, CO 23/112. See also, Stanley to Officer Administering, etc., 15 June 1842, *id.*, at CO 24/22.

76. In his dispatch of 16 April to the Secretary of State, *supra* note 63, the US consul stated that the individual in question was not a signatory to the New Orleans Protest. In this, he was mistaken. See January 1842 Senate Doc., *supra* note 8, at p. 46. The judges were not alone in viewing the veracity of the New Orleans Protest with extreme skepticism. For instance, in forwarding its text to the foreign secretary, the British minister in Washington had remarked: "It contains, apparently, much falsehood and exaggeration; but it is to be remarked that the Protest is principally directed, not versus England, but versus the American insurance companies at New Orleans and in Virginia, in order to show that the officers and crew did all that depended upon them to prevent the loss of the so called property, by the liberation of the negroes." Fox to Aberdeen, 25 February 1842, *supra* note 49.

77. *Supra* note 63.

78. The *Weekly Ohio State Journal, supra* note 70, reported that "were the captain, crew, and passengers . . . here present to testify in this case, they should consider them as not entitled to belief or credit, and should charge the jury to that effect." In another report, the chief justice is said to have remarked that those who had signed the protest "ought not to be believed under oath, and that he could not believe them." *Supra* note 71.

79. Webster to Ashburton, 4 May 1842, National Archives, London, FO 5/379.

80. Webster to Everett, 16 May 1842, reproduced in Curtis, *Life of Daniel Webster,* vol. 2, p. 99, at p. 100.

81. *Id.*

3. The *Creole* Incident in Anglo-American Diplomacy

1. See, e.g., Jervey and Huber, "The *Creole* Affair," p. 196, at p. 205.

2. See, e.g., J. C., "Case of the Creole," pp. 79–110.

3. Webster to Tyler, 18 January 1842, in "Message from the President of the United States: In Compliance with a Resolution of the Senate, Copies of Correspondence in Relation to the Mutiny on Board the Brig Creole, and the Liberation of the Slaves Who Were Passengers in the Said Vessel," 27th Congress, 2d Session, Senate, January 1842 [hereafter January 1842 Senate Doc.], p. 1.

4. Webster to Everett, 29 January 1842, in *Correspondence with Foreign Powers Not Parties to Conventions Giving Right of Search of Vessels Suspected of the Slave Trade: 1842* (HMSO, London, 1843): p. 161, at p. 161.

5. Fox to Aberdeen, 25 February 1842 (received March 26), *id.*, p. 160. The text of the Webster to Everett dispatch thereafter became the focus of scholarly attention on both sides of the Atlantic. See, e.g., Jay, *The Creole Case and Mr. Webster's Despatch;* and Phillimore, *The Case of the Creole Considered in a Second Letter to the Right Hon*

Lord Ashburton. See also Giddings, *History of the Rebellion: Its Author and Causes,* at pp. 173–79, for a discussion of the Congressional debate at that time. For an influential early contribution to the legal literature, see Wheaton, "Examen des questions de jurisdiction qui se sont élevées entre les gouvernements anglais et américan, dans l'affaire de la Créole," *Revue etrangere et francaise,* vol. 9 (1842): p. 345 *et seq.* See also Wheaton, *Elements of International Law,* at p. 139.

6. *Supra* note 4, p. 162.

7. *Id.*, p. 161.

8. *Id.*, pp. 161–62.

9. *Id.*, p. 163.

10. See, e.g., *id.*, at pp. 162–63. In particular, Webster believed that by the time they were returned to the US and proceedings instituted, "the witnesses might be scattered across half the globe," *id.*, 163. This stance caused some controversy when it became known in the US Senate. See, e.g., *supra* note 1, at p. 205. As Webster was to explain to Everett on 28 June 1842, "we do not demand the restitution of fugitive slaves; that, without treaty stipulations to that effect, we do not demand, and shall not demand, the surrender of fugitives fleeing from justice." Dispatch reproduced in Curtis, *Life of Daniel Webster,* vol. 2, at pp. 104–7.

11. *Supra* note 4, 164.

12. *Id.*

13. *Id.*, p. 162.

14. Wiltse, "Daniel Webster and the British Experience," p. 58, at p. 66.

15. Greenwood, "Caroline, The," para. 1.

16. See, e.g., *supra* note 14, at pp. 66–67.

17. Lower, "An Unpublished Letter of Daniel Webster," p. 360, at p. 360.

18. See *supra* note 14, at p. 69.

19. *Id.*, p. 71.

20. See, e.g., Chadwick, *The Creole Rebellion: The Most Successful Slave Revolt in American History,* at pp. 83–86.

21. *Supra* note 14, p. 73.

22. *Supra* note 20, p. 112.

23. See, e.g., Orbell, "Baring, Alexander, first Baron Ashburton."

24. See *id.*

25. See Ashburton to Aberdeen, 22 December 1841, in British Library, London, Aberdeen Papers, Add MS 43123 (1841–1846) [hereafter Aberdeen Papers].

26. Cockburn to Stanley, 17 November 1841, National Archives, London, CO 23/110 and received in the Colonial Office on 27 December. There is nothing to suggest that anything in Ashburton's background would have disqualified him from selection had the *Creole* been on the agenda from the outset. Though he received some financial benefit from the abolition of slavery, Orbell (*supra* note 23) describes his attitude to enslavement

as "ambivalent." On compensation, see "Alexander Baring: Profile and Legacy Summary," Centre for the Study of the Legacies of British Slavery, at ch. 1, note 27, above.

27. Aberdeen to Fox, 3 January 1842, Aberdeen Papers.

28. Fox to Aberdeen, 29 January 1842, Aberdeen Papers.

29. See *supra* note 4, at p. 162.

30. See, e.g., note of 14 February 1842 initialed by Lord Aberdeen, Aberdeen Papers.

31. See the memorandum of the Duke of Wellington on Lord Ashburton's instructions, 8 February 1842, held in the Aberdeen Papers. The duke was the leader of the House of Lords at the time and had been much consulted on the special mission by the foreign secretary.

32. This had been sent by the British minister in Washington to the foreign secretary on 25 February 1842. See *supra* note 5. It is marked as having been received only on 26 March. As the text had been published in the American press it is, of course, possible that it may have come to the attention of the authorities in London at an earlier stage by an alternative route.

33. Aberdeen to Ashburton, 3 March 1842, Aberdeen Papers.

34. *Id.*

35. They were not finally settled for several weeks. See, e.g., Aberdeen to Ashburton, 1 April 1842, Aberdeen Papers. See also Adams, "Lord Ashburton and the Treaty of Washington," p. 764, at p. 764.

36. See Everett to Aberdeen, 1 March 1842, reproduced in *supra* note 4, at pp. 115–23. The enclosures to that protest are also reproduced. See p. 123 *et seq.* In mid-April the Foreign Secretary indicated to the American envoy why he was unable to acquiesce in that claim. See Aberdeen to Everett, 18 April 1842, in *id.*, at pp. 193–96.

37. The American envoy had occasion to return to the issues of international law engaged, in the view of his government, by the facts of the *Creole.* This took the form of a diplomatic protest submitted in early May over the actions of the colonial authorities in the Bahamas in the October 1840 case of the *Hermosa* which had been wrecked on Spanish Key near Abaco. The enslaved persons aboard had then been liberated by those authorities. The duties imposed by the Law of Nations on Great Britain in both instances were deemed by his government to be the same. As he opined, "the Government of the United States cannot admit that the vessels of a friendly power, driven by stress of weather or by mutiny into Her Majesty's ports, can in consequence of a change in the municipal law of England [here the 'Emancipation' Act], be rightfully deprived of any aid and assistance to which they are entitled by the law and comity of nations." Everett to Aberdeen, 3 May 1842, National Archives, London, FO 84/423.

38. *Supra* note 14, p. 74. The secretary of state would subsequently remark to his envoy in London: "Lord Ashburton has been received here with much kindness, by the Government and the public. His personal demeanor makes friends, and we all think he has come with an honest and sincere intent of removing all causes of jealousy, disquietude,

or difference between the two countries, and certainly do not suppose a better selection could have been made." Webster to Everett, 25 April 1842, Aberdeen Papers.

39. Also known as St John's Church Parish House.

40. *Supra* note 1, p. 207.

41. *Supra* note 35, pp. 770–71.

42. National Archives, London, FO 84/423.

43. This is considered in chapter 4 below.

44. At the conclusion of the negotiations, Ashburton wrote that "[t]he Secretary of State behaved well and liberally throughout." Ashburton to Aberdeen, 9 August 1842, Aberdeen Papers.

45. Ashburton to Aberdeen, 29 June 1842, Aberdeen Papers. See also Jones, "The Influence of Slavery on the Webster–Ashburton Negotiations," p. 48, at p. 49. See also p. 58, where he concludes more generally that the slavery issue had "poisoned the atmosphere."

46. Ashburton to Aberdeen, 29 May 1842, Aberdeen Papers.

47. *Id.*

48. Adams, *supra* note 35, p. 764.

49. Webster to Ashburton, 4 May 1842, National Archives, London, FO 5/379.

50. Ashburton to Aberdeen, 12 May 1842, National Archives, London, FO 5/379.

51. Ashburton to Aberdeen, 25 April 1842, National Archives, London, FO 84/423.

52. *Id.*

53. *Id.*

54. See Ashburton to Aberdeen, 28 April 1842, National Archives, London, FO 5/379. In the letter he noted: "I was confidentially assured that the whole clause was drawn up by Judge Story, a great authority in this country, but, as he is on the Bench, his name is not to be mentioned." This is a reference to Joseph Story, who had served as a highly influential associate justice of the US Supreme Court since early 1812.

55. The text of the draft clause was attached to the dispatch of 28 April, *id.*

56. *Id.*

57. Aberdeen to Ashburton, 26 May 1842, Aberdeen Papers.

58. Aberdeen to Ashburton, 3 June 1842, Aberdeen Papers.

59. *Id.* The inconvenience of enacting primary legislation to give effect to each and every treaty containing a provision for the return of fugitive offenders to foreign states was addressed in the Extradition Act, 1870, c. 52. See, e.g., Twiss, *The Law of Nations Considered as Independent Political Communities,* vol. 2, at pp. 416–17.

60. Ashburton to Aberdeen, 29 June 1842, National Archives, London, FO 5/379.

61. *Id.*

62. *Id.* President Tyler harbored not dissimilar fears. See, e.g., Jones, *To the Webster-Ashburton Treaty: A Study in Anglo-American Relations, 1783–1843,* at p. 149. On 27 March 1843, the law officers of the Crown (Dodson, Pollock, and Follett) concluded that under existing British law, a slave was considered "capable of committing a crime" and that

consequently, he or she was amenable to extradition for any of the offenses enumerated in the relevant treaty. National Archives, London, FO 83/2207.

63. Namely, satisfying the evidential threshold required by the clause (the *prima facie* case requirement) and the so-called double criminality requirement. The latter aroused some controversy during later Senate consideration. See Boister, "A History of Double Criminality in Extradition," p. 218, at p. 226.

64. Curtis, *supra* note 10, p. 105.

65. Ashburton informed the Foreign Secretary on 9 August: "I have altogether omitted mutiny in any shape. It is a crime most proper to be guarded against in such a Convention, but as the subject gave rise to controversy in considering its possible application to slavery, it has been thought expedient to omit it." Ashburton to Aberdeen, 9 August 1842, National Archives, London, FO 5/380.

66. The treaty was signed by Webster and Ashburton for their respective governments on 9 August 1842. Its formal title is "A Treaty to Settle and Define the Boundaries Between the Territories of the United States and the Possessions of Her Britannic Majesty in North America: For the Final Suppression of the African Slave Trade: and the Giving Up of Criminals Fugitive from Justice, in Certain Cases."

67. It reads, in full, as follows:

> It is agreed that the United States and Her Britannic Majesty shall, upon mutual requisitions by them, or their Ministers, Officers, or authorities, respectively made, deliver up to justice, all persons who, being charged with the crime of murder or assault with intent to commit murder, or Piracy, or arson, or robbery, or Forgery, or the utterance of forged paper, committed within the jurisdiction of either, shall seek an asylum, or shall be found, within the territories of the other: Provided, that this shall only be done upon such evidence of criminality as, according to the laws of the place where the fugitive or person so charged, shall be found, would justify his apprehension and commitment for trial, if the crime or offense had there been committed: And the respective Judges and other Magistrates of the two Governments, shall have power, jurisdiction, and authority, upon complaint made under oath, to issue a warrant for the apprehension of the fugitive or person so charged, that he may be brought before such Judges or other Magistrates, respectively, to the end that the evidence of criminality may be heard and considered, and if, on such hearing, the evidence be deemed sufficient to sustain the charge it shall be the duty of the examining Judge or Magistrate, to certify the same to the proper Executive Authority, that a warrant may issue for the surrender of such fugitive. The expense of such apprehension and delivery shall be borne and defrayed by the Party who makes the requisition, and receives the fugitive.

68. Ashburton to Webster, 9 August 1842, in (1841–1842) *BFSP,* vol. 30, p. 367.

69. See An Act for Giving Effect to a Treaty Between Her Majesty and the United

States of America for the Apprehension of Certain Offenders, 1843, chapter 76. For a brief discussion of its operation in practice, see Wheaton, *Elements of International Law,* at pp. 155–56.

70. See Message from the President of the United States to the Senate of the United States of 11 August 1842, Transmitting a Treaty with Great Britain, 27th Congress, 3d Session, House (Exec. Doc. No. 2), at p. 22.

71. *Id.*

72. Ashburton to Aberdeen, 25 April 1842, National Archives, London, FO 84/423. This concern was reinforced upon receipt of news of the American protest in relation to the *Hermosa* considered in note 37 above. On June 14, he warned Aberdeen of the likely repetition of such incidents. He continued, "If we wish to live in harmony with a powerful and very sensitive neighbour, we must consider something more than our rights." Aberdeen to Ashburton, 14 June 1842, National Archives, London, FO 5/379.

73. Ashburton to Aberdeen, 25 April 1842, *id.*

74. See *id.*

75. National Archives, London, FO 5/379.

76. Aberdeen to Ashburton, 26 May 1842, Aberdeen Papers.

77. Ashburton to Aberdeen, 29 June 1842, National Archives, London, FO 5/379.

78. *Id.*

79. Curtis, *supra* note 10, pp. 105–6.

80. *Supra* note 77.

81. *Id.*

82. *Id.*

83. "Lord Ashburton's Suggestions to Mr. Webster on the Creole Case," appended to *id.*

84. Ashburton to Aberdeen, 9 August 1842, Aberdeen Papers. See also Jones, *supra* note 45, at pp. 51–52. The word "revision" is unclear in the source.

85. Ashburton to Aberdeen, *id.* See further in Jones, "The Peculiar Institution and National Honor: The Case of the *Creole* Slave Revolt," p. 28, at pp. 44–45.

86. Webster to Ashburton, 1 August 1842, *supra* note 70, p. 114.

87. *Id.,* p. 120.

88. Ashburton to Webster, 6 August 1842, reproduced in *id.,* at pp. 120–22.

89. *Id.,* p. 120. In subsequent state practice, the USA on occasion invoked one or more of the formulations of the international law "distress" rule advanced by Webster during the *Creole* negotiations; for example, it was advanced as a precedent by then Secretary of State Bayard in the context of the treatment of the fishing vessel *Marion Grimes* by the authorities of Nova Scotia in 1886. See Bayard to Phelps, 6 November 1886, in *Papers Relating to the Foreign Relations of the United States, Transmitted to Congress, with the Annual Message of the President, December 6, 1886* (Washington, DC: US Government Printing Office, 1887): pp. 363–70. It was acknowledged, however, that Ashburton "had

questioned the applicability of the rule to the case of the *Creole.*" *Id.*, p. 365. The same communication cited, with approval, the 1855 arbitral award in the case of the *Creole* discussed in chapter 4 below.

90. *Id.* In the course of July, Webster involved Hugh S. Legaré, the then attorney general of the United States, in the negotiations with Ashburton, thus adding an extra level of complexity to the consideration of relevant issues of international law. See his Opinion—reduced to writing at Ashburton's insistence—of 20 July 1842 in *Official Opinions by the Attorneys General of the United States,* vol. 4 (Washington, DC: Robert Farnham, 1852): pp. 98–105. This came too late in the process to be subject to discussion with the Foreign Secretary in London prior to the finalization of the exchange of notes in early August relating to the *Creole* incident. Legaré became secretary of state, *ad interim,* in 1843 following Webster's resignation but died shortly thereafter. See, e.g., Maxeiner, "Legaré, Hugh Swinton," p. 427, at p. 428.

91. *Id.*, p. 122; also to be found at National Archives, London, FO 5/380.

92. Webster to Ashburton, 8 August 1842, *id.*, p. 123.

93. *Id.* The exchange of letters has been reproduced elsewhere. See, e.g., Downey, *The Creole Affair: The Slave Rebellion that Led the US and Great Britain to the Brink of War,* appendix 3.

94. Ashburton to Aberdeen, 9 August 1842, Aberdeen Papers.

95. *Id.* See further in Jones, *supra* note 85, at p. 44.

96. Parliamentary Debates, House of Commons, 10 April 1843, col. 747–49.

97. See Cockburn to Stanley, 29 March 1842, National Archives, London, CO 23/112.

98. *Supra* note 96.

99. Stanley to Cockburn, 30 April 1842, National Archives, London, CO 24/22.

100. *Id.*

101. Ashburton to Aberdeen, 9 August 1842, Aberdeen papers.

102. See *id.*

103. See Ashburton to Aberdeen, 13 August 1842, National Archives, London, FO 5/380.

4. Capitalism and Slavery

1. See New Orleans Protest of 7 December 1841, reproduced in "Message from the President of the United States: In Compliance with a Resolution of the Senate, Copies of Correspondence in Relation to the Mutiny on Board the Brig Creole, and the Liberation of the Slaves who Were Passengers in the Said Vessel," 27th Congress, 2d Session, Senate, January 1842 [hereafter January 1842 Senate Doc], pp. 36–46.

2. *Id.*, 46.

3. Johnson, "White Lies: Human Property and Domestic Slavery Aboard the Slave Ship *Creole,*" p. 237, at p. 243.

4. J. C., "Case of the Creole," p. 79, at p. 104.

5. Comment contained in his Note of the Judgment of the Creole case in April 1842 reproduced in appendix 2.

6. Fox to Aberdeen, 25 February 1842, reproduced in *Correspondence with Foreign Powers Not Parties to Conventions Giving Right of Search of Vessels Suspected of the Slave Trade: 1842* (London: HMSO, 1843): p. 160.

7. Levy, *Freaks of Fortune: The Emerging World of Capitalism and Risk in America*, p. 21.

8. Schafer, *Slavery, the Civil Law, and the Supreme Court of Louisiana*, p. 164.

9. All were heard at first instance in the Commercial Court; all were then appealed to the Louisiana Supreme Court. See, *McCargo v. New Orleans Insurance Co.*, 10 Rob (LA) 202, (1845); *Andrews v. Ocean Insurance Co.*, 10 Rob (LA) 332, (1845); *Lockett v. Fireman's Insurance Co.*, 10 Rob (LA) 332 (1845); *Hagan v. Ocean Insurance Co.*, 10 Rob (LA) 333 (1845); *Johnson v. Ocean Insurance Co.*, 10 Rob (LA), 334 (1845); *McCargo v. Merchants' Insurance Co.*, 10 Rob (LA) 334 (1845); and *Lockett v. Merchants' Insurance Co.*, 10 Rob (LA) 339 (1845). For a useful summary see Catterall, *Judicial Cases Concerning American Slavery and the Negro*, vol. 3, at pp. 565–68.

10. Levy, *supra* note 7, at p. 30.

11. *Id*, 34.

12. *McCargo v. Merchants' Insurance Co.*, *supra* note 9, at p. 335.

13. See *McCargo v. New Orleans Insurance Co.*, *supra* note 9, at p. 258.

14. A note to the judgment, *id*.

15. *Supra* note 12, p. 335.

16. See, generally, Gilmore, *The Confederate Jurist: The Legal Life of Judah P. Benjamin*, chapter 1.

17. See, generally, Benjamin and Slidell, *Digest of the Reported Decisions of the Superior Court of the Late Territory of Orleans and of the Supreme Court of Louisiana*.

18. Cited, *supra* note 9.

19. *Supra* note 13, p. 312.

20. *Id*.

21. See *id.*, at pp. 259–86.

22. *Supra* note 7, p. 49.

23. See *supra* note 13, at p. 259.

24. *Id.*, p. 260.

25. *Id.*, p. 279.

26. *Id.*, p. 283.

27. Butler, "Judah Philip Benjamin," in Lewis, *Great American Lawyers*, vol. 6, p. 257, at p. 269. This is an apparent reference to the brief for the defendants submitted by Benjamin, Slidell, and Conrad in *Lockett v. Merchants' Insurance Co.*, cited *supra*, note 9.

This was in substantially similar terms to the arguments presented to the Supreme Court of Louisiana by the same Attorneys in *McCargo* v. *New Orleans Insurance Co.*, *op. cit.*

28. *Supra* note 13, p. 314.

29. See *id.*, at pp. 312–14.

30. See, generally, Bonquois, "The Career of Henry Adams Bullard, Louisiana Jurist, Legislator and Educator," p. 999 *et seq.*

31. *Supra* note 13, p. 314.

32. *Id.*, p. 315.

33. *Id.*, p. 318.

34. *Id.*, p. 316. He similarly referenced the unanimous resolution of the US Senate in relation to the *Enterprize*. This is considered below.

35. See *supra* note 3, at p. 243.

36. Examined, in particular, in chapter 1 above.

37. *Supra* note 13, p. 318.

38. *Id.*, p. 325.

39. *Id.*, p. 321.

40. See, e.g., *id.*, at p. 325.

41. *Id.*, p. 326.

42. See, e.g., *id.*, p. 327.

43. *Id.*, p. 327.

44. *Id.*, p. 330.

45. See, *id.*, at pp. 329–30. He did not directly engage with the evidence of the attorney general of the Bahamas alleging that the New Orleans Protest contained several untruths and fabrications. See *id.*, at pp. 251–52.

46. *Id.*, p. 330.

47. *Id.*

48. *Id.*, p. 332.

49. *Id.*

50. *Supra* note 12, p. 337.

51. *Id.*, p. 338. See generally also, *Lockett* v. *Merchants' Insurance Co.*, *supra*, note 9. See further *McCargo* v. *Merchants' Insurance Co.—Lockett v. The Same—Application for a Re-hearing*, 10 Rob (LA) 349 (1845). The application was refused.

52. *Supra* note 7, p. 56.

53. *Supra* note 13, p. 327.

54. See, generally, chapter 3.

55. "Message of the President of the United States Communicating the Proceedings of the Commissioners for the Adjustment of Claims under the Convention with Great Britain of February 8, 1853," 34th Congress, 1st Session, Senate, Ex Doc. No. 103 [hereafter 1856 Senate Doc], pp. ii–iii.

56. The Permanent Court of International Justice (PCIJ) located at The Hague Peace Palace. With the establishment of the United Nations, it became titled the International Court of Justice (ICJ).

57. Merrills and De Brabandere, *Merrills' International Dispute Settlement,* p. 133. Other scholars place emphasis on the Jay Treaty of 1794 between the same countries as the effective modern catalyst for the development of international arbitration. See, e.g., Schwarzenberger, *International Law,* vol. 4, p. 21 *et seq.*

58. For the text see, e.g., National Archives, London, FO 93/8/24.

59. *Id.*, Article V.

60. See *supra* note 55, at p. iv.

61. This was set at one year from the date of first sitting. This was extended by "a period not exceeding four months" by Article I of a Convention of 8 February 1853. See National Archives, London, FO 93/8/29. This treaty thus set a cut-off of no later than 15 January 1855 for the completion of the work of the Commission. The *Creole* Award, appendix 3, is dated 9 January 1855. The judgment in the associated *Hermosa* case was handed down only on 11 January.

62. *John Pemberton, Liquidator of the Merchants' Insurance Co. v. Lockett, Berret, and Johnson* (21) 62 US 257, at p. 263.

63. The US appointed John A. Thomas (1810–1858). A graduate of West Point and a lawyer, he served as a US under secretary of state (1855–1857). The agent for the United Kingdom was James Hannen (1821–1894). Later known as Baron Hannen, he was a barrister and then judge, rising to the rank of lord of appeal in ordinary.

64. Hornby was knighted in 1862.

65. *Supra* note 58, Article I.

66. *Id.*

67. *Supra* note 55, p. 15.

68. See *id.*, at pp. 15–16.

69. *Id.*, p. 455.

70. He had no family connection with the UK. He had, however, briefly served as the American envoy to the Court of St. James (1831–1832).

71. At an earlier stage of his career, he had been intimately involved in pressing the claim of the slavers for loss of "property" on the merchant vessel *Comet* when wrecked off Abaco and securing compensation for them. See, e.g., Law Officers Opinion of 9 April 1834, National Archives, London, FO 83/2346.

72. *Supra* note 55, p. 456.

73. See *id.*, at p. 18.

74. See *id.*, at pp. 457–58.

75. See, e.g., Killick, "Bates, Joshua (10 October 1788–24 September 1864)."

76. *Supra* note 55, p. 457.

77. See *id.*, p. 458.

78. See *id.*, at pp. 458–59.

79. *Id.*, p. 458.

80. To appoint a non-lawyer was by no means unique in this early period of international arbitration. See, e.g., Neff, *Justice Among Nations: A History of International Law,* at p. 329.

81. Kotzur, "Ex aequo et bono," para. 1.

82. See Hornby, *Report of the Proceedings of the Mixed Commission on Private Claims, Established Under the Convention between Great Britain and the United States of America of the 8th February, 1853,* at p. 52.

83. *Supra* note 55, p. 38.

84. *Supra* note 82, p. 388.

85. 1856 Senate Doc., *op. cit.*, p. 236. The text of the Award of 23 December 1854 is at pp. 236–37.

86. See *id.*, p. 236.

87. *Id.*

88. *Id.*, p. 220.

89. See *id.*, p. 237.

90. See, generally, *id.*, at pp. 189–201.

91. *Id.*, pp. 208–9. Note the similarity of this line of reasoning with the unanimous April 1840 Resolution of the US Senate on the law as applicable to the *Enterprize* incident. See Congressional Globe, 26th Congress, 1st Session, p. 327.

92. 1856 Senate Doc., *op. cit.*, pp. 218–19.

93. *Id.*, p. 221.

94. Lord Stowell stated in *The Eleanor,* (1809) Edw 137: "It must be an urgent distress; it must be something of a grave necessity." See also, e.g., *The New York,* 3 Wheat 59 (1818). See further, *infra* note 162, at pp. 200–201. For a modern formulation, see Crawford, *The International Law Commission's Articles on State Responsibility,* p. 174; viz., Draft Art 24(1).

95. 1856 Senate Doc., *op. cit.*, p. 234.

96. *Id.*

97. See *id.*, at pp. 234–35.

98. *Id.*, 221.

99. *Id.*, 223.

100. *Id.*, 224.

101. For a convenient overview of the proceedings and outcome of the case of the *Enterprize*—sometimes incorrectly spelled with an "s" rather than a "z"—see *Yearbook of the International Law Commission,* vol. 2, Part One (1978): pp. 150–51.

102. 1856 Senate Doc., *op. cit.*, p. 237.

103. *Id.*

104. *Id.* The umpire also stated, "No offence was committed against the municipal laws of Great Britain or her colonies. . . ." See *id.*

105. *Id.*

106. Utilizing the rate of exchange used by the Commissioners, this was roughly equivalent to £10,124. According to the online Bank of England CPI calculator, this represents approximately £897,265 in January 2024 terms.

107. As noted in chapter 1 above, the American schooner *Hermosa* with 38 slaves on board was wrecked off Abaco in the Bahamas in 1840, and the slaves were subsequently liberated by the colonial authorities. Umpire Bates, in an Award of 11 January 1855, found in favor of the United States and awarded compensation of $16,000. See *supra* note 55, at pp. 238–40.

108. *Supra* note 82, p. 388. See also p. 385.

109. See *id.*, p. 377.

110. *Id.*

111. *Id.*

112. *Id.*

113. *Id.*, p. 378. As one US legal commentator argued in early 1842: "The fact is that, when the Creole arrived at Nassau, neither she nor the negroes on board of her were in possession of the officers and crew. Far from it. . . . If the negroes were not in custody, it is a contradiction in terms to say that the authorities at Nassau interfered, to set them free." "Postscript," *American Jurist and Law Magazine,* vol. 27 (April 1842): p. 53.

114. See, *supra,* note 82, at p. 378.

115. *Id.*, p. 380.

116. *Id.*, p. 382.

117. *Id.*, p. 384.

118. *Id.*, p. 383.

119. 1824, c. 113.

120. See Punishment of Offences Act, 1837, c. 91.

121. That, in the view of the colonial authorities, this action had not, in law, reduced those on board once more to a state of slavery is implied by the fact that, in contrast to the events surrounding the *Enterprize,* they were not in the event freed via a writ of *habeas corpus.* This was "the course to be pursued generally, when a slave or slaves are known to be on board a foreign vessel in any part of Her Majesty's dominions." Opinion of the Law Officers of the Crown, 28 April 1856, in McNair, *International Law Opinions,* vol. 2, p. 89.

122. See *supra* note 82, at pp. 383–84. See also Phillimore, *Commentaries Upon International Law,* vol. 4, at pp. 15–16.

123. *Supra* note 4, pp. 104–5.

124. See Everett to Aberdeen, 1 March 1842, reproduced at *supra* note 6, pp. 115–23.

125. See *supra* note 1. Bacon, in his evidence in *McCargo* v. *New Orleans Insurance*

Co., *op. cit.*, at pp. 231–33, provided a similar, but somewhat less aggressive, account of events. The wording of the award by Umpire Bates suggests reliance on the former and ignorance of the latter.

126. See *supra* note 1, at p. 44.

127. Gifford, in his evidence in *McCargo* v. *New Orleans Insurance Co.*, *op. cit.*, at p. 214, timed this attempt at "about two hours before the slaves were liberated" on Friday, November 12.

128. *Supra* note 1, p. 45.

129. *Id.* See also the evidence of Bacon, *supra* note 125, at p. 232.

130. *Supra* note 82, p. 384. See also, e.g., the written brief of Slidell, Benjamin and Conrad for the defendants in *Lockett* v. *Merchants' Insurance Co.*, *op. cit.*, at pp. 73–75 of said submission.

131. *Supra* note 82, p. 384. On 29 November 1843 John Nelson, the then attorney general of the United States, opined that the seizure of an American vessel by an American warship within the jurisdiction of a foreign government was a violation of the territorial sovereignty of that foreign state. See Hall, *Official Opinions of the Attorneys General of the United States,* vol. 4, at pp. 285–86. Such a seizure of a merchant vessel by a merchant vessel would, *a fortiori,* constitute a legal wrong.

132. Hornby's view, *supra* note 82, at p. 384, that the "attempt" had never been made is, as a matter of law, open to serious question.

133. *Id.*, p. 385.

134. *Id.*

135. *Id.*, p. 387.

136. This is most clearly evident in his treatment of the plot by the US consul and Captain Woodside to retake the *Creole* by force.

137. At the rate of exchange used by the commission, this came to approximately £22,800. Utilizing the Bank of England CPI calculator, this equates to roughly £2,020,700 in January 2024 terms.

138. See *supra* note 55, at p. 78.

139. See *id.*, at p. iii.

140. *Id.*, p. 260.

141. *Supra* note 57, p. 135. In the words of Kotzur, *supra* note 81, para. 13: "Aiming for compromise and conciliation *extra* or even *contra legem, ex aequo et bono* findings have their roots in moral, social and political spheres, and rely on a flexible rule of reason rather than a strict rule of law. They function as a deliberate corrective of the law."

142. *Supra* note 80, p. 328.

143. See *id.*, at p. 329.

144. See, e.g., Churchill and Lowe, *The Law of the Sea,* at pp. 71–75. The uncertainty surrounding the juridical nature of the territorial sea is well illustrated by *Regina* v. *Keyn* (1876) 2 Ex D 63 which, in turn, prompted the enactment by the UK Parliament of the

Territorial Waters Jurisdiction Act 1878, c. 73. Interestingly, the *Keyn* case was, without doubt, the greatest to involve Judah P. Benjamin in his post-Civil War political exile in London. See Gilmore, *supra* note 16, at pp. 109–14.

145. Lee, "Jurisdiction over Foreign Merchant Ships in the Territorial Sea: An Analysis of the Geneva Convention on the Law of the Sea," p. 77, at p. 80, note 9.

146. See, e.g., Churchill and Lowe, *supra* note 144, at pp. 61–63.

147. *Id.*, p. 66. See also, e.g., *infra* note 154, at pp. 209–12.

148. See, e.g., Colombos, *The International Law of the Sea,* at pp. 320–26.

149. Reproduced in McNair, *supra* note 121, p. 191, at p. 194. In the end, the Conference decided, for reasons of both time and complexity, not to address this issue. See League of Nations, "Acts of the Conference for the Codification of International Law," Vol. 1, Plenary Meetings, Doc. No. C.351.M.145.1930.V, at p. 125.

150. This was a position long held by the UK. See, e.g., Opinion of the Law Officers, 23 December 1868, reproduced *id.*, at pp. 160–61. The Law Officers also cautioned, at p. 161: "It is plain that this jurisdiction, if carried to the limits of extreme right and unrestrained by considerations of comity or convenience, might become vexatious and irritating to foreign powers." See also, e.g., Hall, *A Treatise on the Foreign Powers and Jurisdiction of the British Crown,* at pp. 80–82.

151. (1923) 262 US 100, p. 124.

152. The US Supreme Court stated in 1887: "And so by comity it came to be generally understood among civilized nations that all matters of discipline and all things done on board which affected only the vessel or those belonging to her, and did not involve the peace and dignity of the country or the tranquillity of the port, should be left by the local government to be dealt with by the authorities of the nation to which the vessel belonged, as the laws of that nation or the interests of its commerce should require. But if crimes are committed on board of a character to disturb the peace and tranquillity of the country to which the vessel has been brought, the offenders have never, by comity or usage, been entitled to any exemption from the operation of the local laws for their punishment if the local tribunal see fit to assert their authority." *Wildenhus's Case* (1887) 120 US 1, p. 12.

153. See "Documents Accompanying the President's Message at the Commencement of the Third Session of the Twenty-Seventh Congress: Message from the President of the United States, Transmitting a Treaty with Great Britain," 27th Congress, 3d Session, House, Doc. No. 2, p. 114, at pp. 115–16.

154. One commentator remarked in 1895: "Mr. Webster would have been embarrassed if he had been compelled to prove the legal value of all that he above states to be law by reference to sufficient authority. The amount of authority which could be adduced in favour of his doctrine at that time was distinctly less than that by which it is now supported." Hall, *A Treatise on International Law,* p. 210.

155. See, e.g., Article 18 of the Harvard Draft Convention on Territorial Waters and

the Comments Thereon in *American Journal of International Law,* vol. 23, Special Supplement (1929): p. 243, at p. 245 and pp. 307–28.

156. McDougal and Burke, *The Public Order of the Oceans: A Contemporary International Law of the Sea,* p. 110.

157. See, e.g., Colombos, *supra* note 148, at pp. 329–30; Churchill and Lowe, *supra* note 144, at p. 68; Schwarzenberger, *International Law,* vol. 1, pp. 198–99; Jennings and Watts, *Oppenheim's International Law,* vol. 1, at pp. 624–25.

158. Reproduced in Hackworth, *Digest of International Law,* vol. 2, at p. 277.

159. *Kate A. Hoff (USA) v. United Mexican States,* IV Reports of International Arbitral Awards, p. 444, at p. 447.

160. For a discussion of the continuing relevance of these concepts in the modern law of the sea, see, e.g., Walker, *Definitions for the Law of the Sea,* at pp. 169–75 and pp. 197–205. For the distinction between these concepts see, e.g., Crawford, *supra* note 94, at pp. 170–77.

161. See, e.g., Van Dyke, "Safe Harbour," paras. 12–14.

162. Jessup, *The Law of Territorial Waters and Maritime Jurisdiction,* p. 194.

163. See *supra* note 55, at p. 190 and pp. 193–96.

164. Le Moli, "'Parity with All Nations': The 'Coolie' Trade and the Quest for Recognition by China and Japan," p. 879, at p. 890.

165. Crawford, "The Maria Luz Affair," p. 583, at p. 587.

166. See Colombo, *Justice and International Law in Meiji Japan: The María Luz Incident and the Dawn of Modernity,* pp. 94–95.

167. See, e.g., Merrills and De Brabandere, *supra* note 57, at p. 133.

168. See *id.* See also Brower, "Arbitration," para. 48.

169. See Brower, *id.*

170. This is implied by the terms of the award. Le Moli, *supra* note 164, at p. 893, suggests that the award was in fact prepared by F. F. de Martens (spelled variously). This seems highly probable as he was familiar with issues of consular jurisdiction in the East and was at the time an adviser to the imperial government. However, the author has seen no direct proof of his involvement in this matter. He was a leading international law scholar and pioneer in the development of international arbitration. See, generally, "Editorial Comment: Frederic de Martens," *American Journal of International Law* 3 (1909): pp. 983–85.

171. See *supra* note 166, at p. 101.

172. See, e.g., *id.*, at p. 105.

173. Charteris, "The Legal Position of Merchantmen in Foreign Ports and National Waters," p. 45, at pp. 85–86.

174. *Supra* note 162, p. 204.

175. Jennings and Watts, *supra* note 157, p. 624.

176. *Supra* note 155, p. 299.

177. *Supra* note 159, p. 447.

178. (1933–1934) *Annual Digest,* Case No. 87, p. 202, at p. 208.

179. See, e.g., Lenoir, "Criminal Jurisdiction Over Foreign Merchant Ships," *Tulane Law Review* 10 (1935–1936): p. 13, at p. 34.

180. *Supra* note 155, at p. 299.

181. For American authority that the general rule of port state jurisdiction extends to the prevention of criminal conduct as well as punishment of offenses which have taken place see *id.*, at p. 309.

182. *Supra* note 124, at p. 119.

183. See *supra* note 153, at p. 119: "Unless they commit, while in port, some act against the laws of the place, they will be permitted to receive supplies, to repair damages, and to depart unmolested."

184. Reproduced in Hall, *supra* note 131, at pp. 98–105. Given the late July date, this did not permit Lord Ashburton to consult with London as to its contents prior to the conclusion of the negotiations.

185. *Id.*, p. 104.

186. *Supra* note 124, p. 119.

187. It is beyond doubt that the abolition of slavery in the Bahamas—and elsewhere within the British Empire—marked an important shift in domestic legal classification from "property" to "person." Consequently, the holding of a person in involuntary bondage also shifted; from the domain of the civil law to that of the criminal law, thus potentially triggering this exception to the distress rule. This is arguably highly relevant in distinguishing the pre-emancipation cases of the *Comet* (1831) and the *Enconium* (1833) from the post-abolition incidents of the *Enterprize, Hermosa* and *Creole* which came before Bates for decision. In the two earlier cases—both of which related to slaves on board American vessels liberated by Bahamian authorities—the British eventually paid compensation to the US. For a brief summary of the two earlier incidents see, e.g., Moore, *A Digest of International Law,* vol. 2, at pp. 350–51. See also, "Indemnities for Slaves On Board the Comet and the Enconium," 27th Congress, 2d Session, House, Doc. No. 242; and "Message of the President of the United States with Copies of Correspondence in Relation to the Seizure of Slaves on Board the Brigs 'Enconium' and 'Enterprize,'" 24th Congress, 2d Session, Senate, Exec. Doc. 174.

188. It is curious that the concepts of consent and acquiescence (including as implied by silence) which were so emphasized by Governor Cockburn in November 1841, as seen in chapter 1, should have played no significant role in those arbitration proceedings. The American view was well articulated by Everett in his formal protest to Aberdeen of 1 March 1842, *supra* note 124, at p. 119: "In the case of the '*Creole,*' the material character of the wrong is not changed by the fact that the soldiers and civil officers were on board the vessel at the request of the commanding officer and the American Consul. They were so indeed, but for a specific purpose, viz.: to arrest the mutineers and to prevent the slaves

from landing. Their presence for any different purpose, especially for any opposite purpose, was not asked, and therefore not lawful."

189. See, e.g., Wheaton, *Elements of International Law,* note 62, at pp. 139–40.

190. See Piggott, *Nationality Including Naturalization and English Law on the High Seas and Beyond,* Part 2, at pp. 32–33.

191. See O'Connell, *The International Law of the Sea,* vol. 2, at pp. 854–55.

192. Corbett, *Leading Cases in International Law,* vol. 1, p. 295.

193. Kämmerer, "Comity," para. 1. See also *id.,* para. 10.

194. See, e.g., Everett to Aberdeen, 1 March 1842, *supra* note 124, at p. 118. See also Webster to Everett, 29 January, reproduced in *id.,* at pp. 161–64. Somewhat tighter formulations were used in the exchange of notes accompanying the Webster–Ashburton Treaty. See, e.g., Webster to Ashburton, 1 August 1842, *supra* note 153, at p. 115: "the rule of law, and the comity and practice of nations."

5. Concluding Reflections

1. See, e.g., Chadwick, *The Creole Rebellion: The Most Successful Slave Revolt in American History,* at p. 93.

2. Levine, Stauffer, and McKivigan, *The Heroic Slave: A Cultural and Critical Edition,* pp. xii–xiii.

3. See, e.g., *id.,* at p. xiii.

4. As articulated in the subtitle of Downey, *The Creole Affair: The Slave Rebellion that Led the US and Great Britain to the Brink of War.*

5. Everett to Aberdeen, 1 March 1842, in *Correspondence with Foreign Powers not Parties to Conventions Giving Right of Search of Vessels Suspected of the Slave Trade: 1842* (London: HMSO, 1843): p. 115, at p. 123. He borrowed this wording directly from instructions from the secretary of state. See, Webster to Everett, 29 January 1842, *id.,* p. 161, at p. 164.

6. Levy, *Freaks of Fortune: The Emerging World of Capitalism and Risk in America,* p. 27.

7. Jones, "The Peculiar Institution and National Honor: The Case of the *Creole* Slave Revolt," p. 28, at p. 48.

8. See Art. I(9) of the UK-US Extradition Convention of 12 July 1889, reproduced in Malloy, *Treaties, Conventions, International Acts, Protocols and Agreements, 1776–1909,* vol. 1, at pp. 740–42.

9. See "Documents Accompanying the President's Message at the Commencement of the Third Session of the Twenty-Seventh Congress: Message from the President of the United States, Transmitting a Treaty with Great Britain," 27th Congress, 3d Session, House, Doc. No. 2, at p. 22.

10. President Tyler's letter of submittal of 11 August 1842 on this point reads as follows: "On the subject of the interference of the British authorities in the West Indies, a

confident hope is entertained that the correspondence which has taken place, showing the grounds taken by this Government, and the engagements entered into by the British minister, will be found such as to satisfy the just expectation of the people of the United States." *Id.*, p. 23.

11. See, generally, Forcese, *Destroying the Caroline: The Frontier Raid that Reshaped the Right to War.*

12. He was tried and acquitted primarily on the basis of alibi evidence.

13. Webster used the following description: "It will be for [Her Majesty's Government] to show a necessity of self-defence, instant, overwhelming, leaving no choice of means, and no moment for deliberation. It will be for it to show, also, that the local authorities of Canada, even supposing the necessity of the moment authorized them to enter the territories of the United States at all, did nothing unreasonable or excessive, since the act, justified by the necessity of self-defence, must be limited by that necessity, and kept clearly within it." Extract of a letter from Webster to Fox, 24 April 1841, enclosed with Webster to Ashburton, 27 July 1842, reproduced in *supra* note 9, p. 123, at p. 128. On July 28, Ashburton informed the Secretary of State "that we are perfectly agreed as to the general principles of international law applicable to this unfortunate case." *Id.*, p. 130, at p. 131.

14. See, e.g., Jennings, "The Caroline and McLeod Cases," p. 82 *et seq.*

15. See, generally, Wood, "The Caroline Incident—1837," pp. 5–16.

16. See Hornby, *Report of the Proceedings of the Mixed Commission on Private Claims Established Under the Convention between Great Britain and the United States of America of the 8th February, 1853,* pp. 455.

17. Webster to Everett, 27 April 1843, in British Library, London, Aberdeen Papers, Add. MS 43123 (1841–1846) [hereafter Aberdeen Papers].

18. Howe, "Everett, Edward (11 April 1794–15 January 1865)."

19. Everett to Aberdeen, 15 September 1842, Aberdeen Papers.

20. He also appears to have been irritated by not being informed by the British authorities as to further developments concerning the progress of the treaty towards entry into force. See, e.g., Ashburton to Aberdeen, 24 October 1842, Aberdeen Papers.

21. Aberdeen to Ashburton, 26 October 1842, Aberdeen Papers.

22. See *id.*

23. See Ashburton to Aberdeen, 27 October 1842, Aberdeen Papers.

24. 10 Rob (LA) 202 (1845).

25. See, generally, Bonquois, "The Career of Henry Adams Bullard, Louisiana Jurist, Legislator and Educator," p. 999 *et seq.*

26. French, *Memoir of Hon Henry A Bullard, LL.D., President of the Louisiana Historical Society, and Late Judge of the Supreme Court of Louisiana,* p. 7.

27. See, e.g., Gilmore, *The Confederate Jurist: The Legal Life of Judah P. Benjamin,* at pp. 14–15.

28. "In Memoriam," *Reports in the Supreme Court of Louisiana*, vol. 36 (1884): p. v, at p. vi.

29. See, generally, Meade, *Judah P. Benjamin: Confederate Statesman*.

30. Reproduced in full in appendix 3.

31. It also references, in passing, the British emancipation legislation which brought freedom to the enslaved population of the Bahamas in 1834.

32. Orbell, "Bates, Joshua (1788–1864)."

33. See, e.g., Jennings and Watts, *Oppenheim's International Law*, vol. 1, at p. 981.

34. See "Draft Conclusions on Identification and Legal Consequences of Peremptory Norms of General International Law (*jus cogens*) 2022," adopted by the International Law Commission at its seventy-third session, in 2022, and submitted to the General Assembly as a part of the Commission's report covering the work of that session (A/77/10, para. 43), Conclusion 2, Conclusion 23, and Annex at (f). By virtue of this status, rules of customary international law inconsistent with it cease to exist to the extent of that inconsistency, *id.*, Conclusion 14(2). See further in *id.*, at p. 88. The report of the Commission will appear in *Yearbook of the International Law Commission 2022*, vol. 2, Part Two (forthcoming). See also Taldi, *The International Law Commission's Draft Conclusions on Peremptory Norms*. To categorize the prohibition of slavery in this manner is far from unusual. See, e.g., Lowe, *International Law*, at p. 59.

35. Churchill and Lowe, *The Law of the Sea*, p. 68.

36. See the discussion in chapter 4 above.

37. See, e.g., Everett to Aberdeen, 1 March 1842, *supra* note 5, at pp. 121–22.

38. "Message of the President of the United States Communicating the Proceedings of the Commissioners for the Adjustment of Claims Under the Convention with Great Britain of February 8, 1853," 34th Congress, 1st Session, Senate, Ex Doc. No. 103, at pp. 205–6.

39. *Id*, p. 203.

40. On the basis of the exchange rate used by the commission, this equated to approximately £36,230. Utilizing the Bank of England CPI calculator, this represents nearly £3,211,000 in January 2024 terms. For a resulting claim concerning the distribution of compensation awarded in the case of the *Creole*, see *Pemberton v. Lockett et al.* 68 US 257 (1858).

41. See, e.g., the "CARICOM Ten Point Plan for Reparatory Justice" available at https://caricom.org/caricom-ten-point-plan-for-reparatory-justice/. On 26 October 2024, the Samoa Communiqué of the Commonwealth Heads of Government Meeting, having discussed the issue of reparatory justice, "agreed that the time has come for a meaningful, truthful and respectful conversation towards forging a common future based on equity." Commonwealth Secretariat, London, Doc. HGM (24) (7), para. 22. See also, e.g., Schwarz, *Reparations for Slavery in International Law*.

42. See, e.g., the glowing characterization of his conduct as umpire by the noted

scholar J. B. Moore in 1898 and reproduced in Scott, *Cases on International Law*, at p. 255, note 1.

43. See *supra* note 32.

44. See, generally, Kerr-Ritchie, *Rebellious Passage: The Creole Revolt and America's Coastal Slave Trade.*

45. *Supra* note 2, p. xxxv.

46. Published in the spring of 1853 as part of a volume entitled *Autographs for Freedom* and edited by Julia Griffiths. It has been frequently republished and has generated much scholarly interest in a range of disciplines. See, e.g., Hoepker, "Frederick Douglass's *The Heroic Slave*—Risk, Fiction and Insurance in Antebellum America," pp. 441–62.

47. *Supra* note 2, xxxvi.

48. "Dreadful Storm at Madeira," *The Observer*, 21 November 1842, p. 1.

49. "The Late Storm at Madeira," *The Times*, 22 November 1842, p. 4. As the same writer explained, the Pontinha is "a jetty, partly natural and partly artificial, which stretches out at the western extremity of Funchal about 150 yards into the sea and terminates in a massive rock crowned by a fort bearing the same name."

50. *Id.*

51. *Supra* note 7, p. 49.

52. Jervey and Huber, "The *Creole* Affair," p. 196, at p. 208.

Appendix 1

1. In the various authorities quoted in Story's *Conflict of Laws*, 520. [Original note.]

2. *R.* v. *Kimberley*, 1 Barnardiston 225; 2 Strange 848; 2 Ventris 314; 3 Keble 785; *Mure* v. *Kaye*, 4 Taunt. 43; *East India Co.* v. *Campbell*, 1 Ves. Senr 246. [Original note.]

3. Stat. 37 Geo. III, c. 13; 42 Geo. III, c. 92. [Original note.]

4. See 2nd Summary Reports 486; 22 American Jurist 350; and Story's *Conflict of Laws*, 520. [Original note.]

Select Bibliography

Books

Benjamin, J. P., and T. Slidell. *Digest of the Reported Decisions of the Superior Court of the Late Territory of Orleans and of the Supreme Court of Louisiana.* New Orleans: J. F. Carter, 1834.

Catterall, H. T., ed. *Judicial Cases Concerning American Slavery and the Negro.* Washington, DC: Carnegie Institution, 1932.

Chadwick, B. *The "Creole" Rebellion: The Most Successful Slave Revolt in American History.* Albuquerque: University of New Mexico Press, 2022.

Churchill, R. R., and A. V. Lowe. *The Law of the Sea.* 3rd ed. Manchester University Press, 1999.

Colombo, G. F. *Justice and International Law in Meiji Japan: The María Luz Incident and the Dawn of Modernity.* Routledge, 2023.

Colombos, C. J., *The International Law of the Sea.* 6th Rev. Ed. Longmans, 1967.

Corbett, P. *Leading Cases in International Law.* 4th ed. London: Sweet and Maxwell, 1922.

Crawford, J., ed. *The International Law Commission's Articles on State Responsibility.* Cambridge University Press, 2002.

Curtis, G. T. *Life of Daniel Webster.* D. Appleton & Co., 1870.

Dale, W. *The Modern Commonwealth.* Butterworths, 1983.

Downey, A. T. *The Creole Affair: The Slave Rebellion that Led the US and Great Britain to the Brink of War.* Rowman & Littlefield, 2014.

Forcese, C. *Destroying the Caroline: The Frontier Raid that Reshaped the Right to War.* Irwin Law, 2018.

French, B. F. *Memoir of Hon Henry A. Bullard, LL.D., President of the Louisiana Historical Society, and Late Judge of the Supreme Court of Louisiana.* 1851. [Retrieved from the Library of Congress, www.loc.gov/item /11008381/].

Giddings, J. R. *History of the Rebellion: Its Author and Causes.* Follett, Foster & Co., 1864.

Gilbert, G. *Transnational Fugitive Offenders in International Law: Extradition and Other Mechanisms.* M. Nijhoff, 1998.

Gilmore, W. C. *The Confederate Jurist: The Legal Life of Judah P. Benjamin.* Edinburgh University Press, 2021.

Hackworth, G. H. *Digest of International Law.* US Government Printing Office, 1941.

Hall, B. F., ed. *Official Opinions of the Attorneys General of the United States.* Robert Farnham, 1852.

Hall, W. E. *A Treatise on International Law.* Clarendon Press, 1895.

———. *A Treatise on the Foreign Powers and Jurisdiction of the British Crown.* Clarendon Press, 1894.

Hornby, E., ed. *Report of the Proceedings of the Mixed Commission on Private Claims, Established Under the Convention between Great Britain and the United States of America of the 8th February, 1853.* London: Harrison and Sons, 1856.

Jay, W. *The Creole Case and Mr. Webster's Despatch.* New-York American, 1842.

Jennings, R., and Watts, A., eds., *Oppenheim's International Law.* 9th ed. Longmans, 1992.

Jessup, P. C. *The Law of Territorial Waters and Maritime Jurisdiction.* G. A. Jennings Co., 1927.

Jones, H. *Mutiny on the Amistad: The Saga of a Slave Revolt and its Impact on American Abolition, Law and Diplomacy.* Oxford University Press, 1987.

———. *To the Webster–Ashburton Treaty: A Study in Anglo-American Relations, 1783–1843.* University of North Carolina Press, 1977.

Kelley, S. M. *American Slavers: Merchants, Mariners, and the Trans-Atlantic Commerce in Captives, 1644–1865.* Yale University Press, 2023.

Kerr-Ritchie, J. R. *Rebellious Passage: The Creole Revolt and America's Coastal Slave Trade.* Cambridge University Press, 2019.

Levine, R. S., Stauffer, J., and McKivigan, J. R. eds. *The Heroic Slave: A Cultural and Critical Edition.* Yale University Press, 2015.

Levy, J. *Freaks of Fortune: The Emerging World of Capitalism and Risk in America*. Harvard University Press, 2012.

Lowe, A. V. *International Law*. Oxford University Press, 2007.

Malloy, W. M. *Treaties, Conventions, International Acts, Protocols and Agreements 1776–1909*. Government Printing Office, 1910.

McDougal, M. S., and Burke, W. T. *The Public Order of the Oceans: A Contemporary International Law of the Sea*. Yale University Press, 1962.

McNair, A. D., ed. *International Law Opinions*. Cambridge University Press, 1956.

Meade, R. D. *Judah P. Benjamin: Confederate Statesman*. Reprint. Louisiana State University Press, 2001.

Merrills, J. and De Brabandere, E. *Merrills' International Dispute Settlement*. 7th ed. Cambridge University Press, 2022.

Moore, J. B. *A Digest of International Law*. Government Printing Office, 1906.

Morriss, R., and W. J. Cooper Jr. *Cockburn and the British Navy in Transition: Admiral Sir George Cockburn, 1772–1853*. University of South Carolina Press, 1998.

Neff, S. C. *Justice Among Nations: A History of International Law*. Harvard University Press, 2014.

O'Connell, D. P. *The International Law of the Sea*. Clarendon Press, 1984.

O'Connell, D. P. and Riordon, A., eds. *Opinions on Imperial Constitutional Law*. Law Book Co., 1971.

Phillimore, R. *Commentaries Upon International Law*. 3rd ed. Butterworths, 1859.

———. *The Case of the Creole Considered in a Second Letter to the Right Hon Lord Ashburton*. London: J. Hatchard and Son, 1842.

Piggott, F. *Nationality Including Naturalization and English Law on the High Seas and Beyond*. W. Clowes and Sons, 1907.

Roberts-Wray, K. *Commonwealth and Colonial Law*. London: Stevens & Sons, 1966.

Schafer, J. K. *Slavery, the Civil Law, and the Supreme Court of Louisiana*. Louisiana State University Press, 1994.

Schwarz, K. *Reparations for Slavery in International Law*. Oxford University Press, 2022.

Schwarzenberger, G. *International Law*. Vol. 1. Stevens and Sons, 1957.

———. *International Law*. Vol. 4. Stevens and Sons, 1986.

Scott, J. B., ed. *Cases on International Law.* Boston Book Co., 1902.

Taldi, D. *The International Law Commission's Draft Conclusions on Peremptory Norms.* Oxford University Press, 2024.

Taylor, E. R. *If We Must Die: Shipboard Insurrections in the Era of the Atlantic Slave Trade.* Louisiana State University Press, 2006.

Twiss, T. *The Law of Nations Considered as Independent Political Communities.* 2nd ed. Clarendon Press, 1884.

Walker, G. K., ed. *Definitions for the Law of the Sea: Terms Not Defined by the 1982 Convention.* Leiden: Martinus Nijhoff, 2012.

Watson, A. *Slave Law in the Americas.* University of Georgia Press, 1989.

Wheaton, H. *Elements of International Law.* 1866 (R. H. Dana). Edited with notes by G. G. Wilson. Clarendon Press, 1936.

Williams, E. E. *Capitalism and Slavery.* 3rd ed. Penguin Books, 2022.

Articles, Notes, and Chapters

Adams, E. D. "Lord Ashburton and the Treaty of Washington." *American Historical Review* 17, no. 4 (July 1912): p. 764.

Bantekas, I. "Criminal Jurisdiction of States under International Law." In *Max Planck Encyclopedias of International Law.* Oxford University Press, March 2011.

Boase, G. C. "Dodson, Sir John (1780–1858)." In *Oxford Dictionary of National Biography.* Revised by H. Mooney. Oxford University Press, 23 September 2004.

Boister, N. "A History of Double Criminality in Extradition." *Journal of the History of International Law* 25, no. 2 (June 2023): p. 218.

Bonquois, D. J. "The Career of Henry Adams Bullard, Louisiana Jurist, Legislator and Educator." *Louisiana Historical Quarterly* 23 (1940): p. 999.

Brower, C. H. "Arbitration." *Max Planck Encyclopedias of International Law.* Online edition.

Bush, J. A. "The British Constitution and the Creation of Slavery in America." In *Slavery and the Law,* edited by P. Finkelman. Rowman and Littlefield, 2002.

Butler, P. "Judah Philip Benjamin." In *Great American Lawyers,* vol. 6, edited by W. D. Lewis. John C. Winston Co., 1909.

Cairns, J. W. "After *Somerset:* The Scottish Experience." *Journal of Legal History* 33, no. 3, (2012): p. 291.

Charteris, A. H. "The Legal Position of Merchantmen in Foreign Ports and National Waters." *British Year Book of International Law* 1 (1920–1921): p. 45.

Crawford, S. J. "The Maria Luz Affair." *The Historian* 46, no. 4 (1984): p. 583.

Finkenbine, R. E. "The Symbolism of Slave Mutiny: Black Abolitionist Responses to the *Amistad* and *Creole* Incidents." In *Rebellion, Repression, Reinvention: Mutiny in Comparative Perspective,* edited by J. Hathaway, p. 233. Praeger, 2001.

Greenwood, C. "Caroline, The," *Max Planck Encyclopedia of International Law.* Online edition.

Hamilton, J. A. "Follett, Sir William Webb (1796–1845)." *Oxford Dictionary of National Biography,* revised by D. Pugsley. Online edition.

Hoepker, K. "Frederick Douglass's *The Heroic Slave*—Risk, Fiction and Insurance in Antebellum America." *American Studies* 60, no. 4 (2015): p. 441.

Howe, D. W. "Everett, Edward (11 April 1794–15 January 1865)." *American National Biography Online.*

J. C. "Case of the Creole." *American Jurist and Law Magazine* 27 (1842): 79.

Jennings, R. Y. "The Caroline and McLeod Cases." *American Journal of International Law* 32, (1938): 82.

Jervey, E. D., and C. H. Huber. "The *Creole* Affair." *Journal of Negro History* 65, no. 3 (1980): p. 196.

Johnson, W. "White Lies: Human Property and Domestic Slavery Aboard the Slave Ship *Creole.*" *Atlantic Studies* 5, no. 2 (2008): p. 237.

Jones, H. "The Peculiar Institution and National Honor: The Case of the *Creole* Slave Revolt." *Civil War History* 21, no. 1 (1975): p. 28.

Jones, W. D. "The Influence of Slavery on the Webster–Ashburton Negotiations." *Journal of Southern History* 22, no. 1 (1956): p. 48.

Kämmerer, J. A. "Comity." *Max Planck Encyclopedias of International Law.* Online edition.

Killick, J. R. "Bates, Joshua (10 October 1788–24 September 1864)." *American National Biography.* Online edition.

Kotzur, M. "Ex aequo et bono." In *Max Planck Encyclopedias of International Law.* Online edition.

Le Moli, G. "'Parity with All Nations': The 'Coolie' Trade and the Quest for

Recognition by China and Japan." *Leiden Journal of International Law* 34 (2021): p. 879.

Lee, L. T. "Jurisdiction Over Foreign Merchant Ships in the Territorial Sea: An Analysis of the Geneva Convention on the Law of the Sea." *American Journal of International Law* 55 (1961): p. 77.

Lenoir, J. J. "Criminal Jurisdiction Over Foreign Merchant Ships." *Tulane Law Review* 10 (1935–1936): p. 13.

Lobban, M. "Twiss, Sir Travers (1809–1897)." *Oxford Dictionary of National Biography.* Online edition.

Lower, A. R. M. "An Unpublished Letter of Daniel Webster." *New England Quarterly* 12, no. 2 (1939): p. 360.

Maxeiner, J. R. "Legaré, Hugh Swinton." In *American National Biography,* vol. 13, p. 427. Oxford University Press, 1999.

McKenna, E. "Cockburn, Sir Francis," *Dictionary of Canadian Biography* 9 (1861–1870). Online edition.

Orbell, J. "Baring, Alexander, First Baron Ashburton." *Oxford Dictionary of National Biography.* Online edition.

———. "Bates, Joshua (1788–1864)." *Oxford Dictionary of National Biography.* Online edition.

Rigg, J. M. "Pollock, Sir (Jonathan) Frederick, First Baronet (1783–1870)." *Oxford Dictionary of National Biography,* revised by P. Polden. Online edition.

Saunders, O. C. "Slave-owners' Compensation: The Bahamas Colony." *International Journal of Bahamian Studies* 25 (2019): p. 45.

Troutman, P., "Grapevine in the Slave Market: African American Geopolitical Literacy and the 1841 *Creole* Revolt." In *The Chattel Principle: Internal Slave Trades in the Americas,* edited by W. Johnson, p. 203. Yale University Press, 2004.

Van Dyke, J. M. "Safe Harbour." *Max Planck Encyclopedias of International Law.* Online edition.

Vega, P. G. "*Creole* Case (1841)." In *Encyclopedia of Emancipation and Abolition in the Transatlantic World,* edited by J. Rodriguez, p. 148. Sharpe Reference, 2007.

Wheaton, H. "Examen des questions de juridiction qui se sont élevées entre les gouvernements anglais et américain, dans l'affaire de la Créole." *Revue etrangere et francaise* 9 (1842): p. 345.

Wiltse, C. M. "Daniel Webster and the British Experience." *Proceedings of the Massachusetts Historical Society* 85 (1973): p. 58.

Wish, H. "American Slave Insurrections before 1861." *Journal of Negro History* 22, no. 3 (1937): p. 299.

Wood, M. "The Caroline Incident—1837." In *The Use of Force in International Law: A Case-Based Approach*, edited by T. Ruys et al., p. 5. Oxford University Press, 2018.

US Congressional Papers

Documents Accompanying the President's Message at the Commencement of the Third Session of the Twenty-Seventh Congress: Message from the President of the United States, Transmitting a Treaty with Great Britain. 27th Congress, 3d Session, House, Doc. No. 2.

Indemnities for Slaves on Board the Comet and Encomium. 27th Congress, 2d Session, House of Representatives, Doc. No. 242.

Message of the President of the United States Communicating the Proceedings of the Commissioners for the Adjustment of Claims Under the Convention with Great Britain of February 8, 1853. 34th Congress, 1st Session, Senate, Exec. Doc. No. 103.

Message from the President of the United States: In Compliance with a Resolution of the Senate, Copies of Correspondence in Relation to the Mutiny on Board the Brig Creole, and the Liberation of the Slaves Who Were Passengers in the Said Vessel. 27th Congress, 2d Session, Senate, January 1842.

Message from the President of the United States to the Senate of the United States of 11 August 1842, Transmitting a Treaty with Great Britain. 27th Congress, 3d Session, House, Exec. Doc. No. 2.

Message of the President of the United States with Copies of Correspondence in Relation to the Seizure of Slaves on Board the Brigs "Enconium" and "Enterprize," 24th Congress, 2d Session, Senate, Exec. Doc. 174.

Index